"While human sin can be a participation insidious twisting of, or idolatrous obses in the created order. In *Music of Darknes*

the Creator, Brian L. Hedrick rightly posits that, 'Music is a good created thing, but when we turn it into the ultimate thing . . . we make it an idol.' Music certainly can be redolent of the truth, goodness and beauty of God, but it is ultimately not God. All those involved with church music, paid or volunteer, need to read and heed this vitally important and engaging book." *—James R. Hart, President, Robert E. Webber Institute for Worship Studies*

"This is a lively and very readable discussion of a vitally important topic. To be released from idolatry is one of the glories of new life in Christ. This book aims to show how and why this is crucial for all Christian musicians."*—Jeremy S. Begbie, Thomas A. Langford Research Professor of Theology, Duke Divinity School; Affiliated Lecturer, Faculties of Divinity and Music, University of Cambridge; Author of* Resounding Truth: Christian Wisdom in the World of Music (Christianity Today *2008 Book Award*)

"Written from the perspective and experience of a pastor and professional musician, Brian Hedrick's *Music of Darkness* deals with a vital question every Christian musician encounters at some point in his or her journey: 'Do I find my identity in my artistic talent and success or in Jesus Christ, who gave me life and talent in the first place?' Hedrick's work is a welcome and necessary addition to the libraries of professional musicians, music educators, students, and those serving in music ministry." *—Joseph R. Crider, Dean of the School of Church Music and Worship, Professor of Church Music and Worship, Southwestern Baptist Theological Seminary*

"Brian Hedrick presents a thoughtful, compelling, and carefully considered diagnosis of musical idolatry, whereby a gift intended for our good and God's glory becomes one of many 'little gods' that vie for our attention and devotion. Hedrick's book provides a helpful corrective for Christ-followers, reminding us to seek first the kingdom of God (Matt. 6:33), to live in harmony with the Holy Spirit and with others (Eph. 4:1-3), and to sing forth the word of Christ with thankfulness and an undivided heart (Col. 3:16, Ps. 86:11-12)." *—Joel S. Davis, Associate Professor of Music, Director of Theory/Composition/Musicology, Samford University School of the Arts; Instrumental Associate, Shades Mountain Baptist Church Worship Arts Ministry*

At the dawn of Time were Three who were One. Creator, Spirit, and Word. As the Spirit hovered over the formless waters, the Creator stretched out his hand, bidding the Word to begin an eternal Music that brought light and form to the universe.

Empty space shifted and became solid. Matter rose green from the elements, and the Spirit breathed into the green matter life but not awareness, and ordained that it should bear seed and spread across the earth suspended in the darkness amidst countless masses of flame and shadow.

Afterward the Creator brought forth creatures not bound by root and soil. They held awareness but lacked will. Governed by the personalities imbued, they spread and multiplied.

The lights were divided, as were the waters, and the seasons. The earth crawled with life given dimension amidst light and shadow. Dew condensed and fell, sprinkling the ground with the scent of life. And the Creator saw that it was good.

But the Creator's vision was yet incomplete, for the most beautiful themes of the Music still roamed the halls of Timelessness. So the Creator descended and walked the fields, gazing at all he had done in so short a span of Time.

He dipped, grabbed a handful of soil, and said to the Word and the Spirit, "Let us make man in our image, after our likeness. And let them have dominion over all living things." So the Creator made man and woman in his image, and said to them, "Be fruitful and multiply, subdue the world and have dominion."

But the man and woman were not satisfied with dominion. They wanted to transcend the boundaries the Creator constructed for them.

They grasped fruit too high for their arms to reach, and ate what they should not have eaten. They became aware of a second Music, of darkness amidst the Light, and they aligned themselves with that second Music, and death entered their forms.

However, even this faltering of steps was planned in the first Music that would sweep up the faltering into a melody more beautiful than any other. The Creator told the man and woman of this coming theme in the first Music, of a babe to issue from the woman's womb—of the one who would be the undoing of death.

Brennan S. McPherson
Prologue, *Flood: The Story of Noah and the Family Who Raised Him*

They exchanged the truth about God for a lie, and worshiped and served created things rather than the Creator—who is forever praised. Amen. (Rom. 1:25, NIV)

Music of Darkness

The Peril of Worshiping the Creation Over the Creator

By Brian L. Hedrick

Foreword by Camp Kirkland

Published in the United States by Nurturing Faith, Macon, GA.
Nurturing Faith is a book imprint of Good Faith Media (goodfaithmedia.org).
Library of Congress Cataloging-in-Publication Data is available.

ISBN: 978-1-63528-134-7

Cover design by Aaron Hedrick

Webber Institute Books

Webber Institute Books (WIB) serves as the publishing arm of the Robert E. Webber Institute for Worship Studies (IWS). The Institute was founded by the late Robert E. Webber for the purpose of forming servant leaders in worship renewal with the perspective that "the way to the future necessarily runs through the past." IWS is the only school in North America dedicated solely to graduate education in biblical foundations, historical development, theological reflection, and cultural analysis of worship. Its vision emphasizes that its graduates will "participate intentionally in the story of the Triune God" to "bring renewal in the local and global church by shaping life and ministry according to that story." In scope it is "gospel-centered in nature and ecumenical in outlook, embracing and serving the whole church in its many expressions and variations." Those interested in obtaining further information concerning the Institute should consult www.iws.edu.

Webber Institute Books are published by agreement with Good Faith Media (www.goodfaithmedia.org) to provide a means for disseminating to the general public varying and differing views concerning the many aspects of worship and Christian life. The ideas expressed in these published materials wholly remain the views of the authors themselves and are not necessarily those of IWS or the publisher.

It is the prayerful concern of both IWS and WIB that the information contained in these works will stimulate further reflection and discussion. The results of such exchange of ideas hopefully will enhance worship renewal within the various segments of the Christian church. Moreover, in keeping with the hopes and dreams of Bob Webber, may all that is done through this publishing enterprise enable Christians to reject the narcissistic patterns prevalent in contemporary society and give the glory to God who sent Jesus, the Christ, to provide for human transformation and in concert provided humans with the divine triune presence through the Holy Spirit.

Contents

Foreword

Anyone who has lived as a believer in Christ knows that it is far too easy to be swayed, diverted, or drawn to "things" that can make us lose sight and devotion to our one true living God. They may even be "good things" that are not necessarily bad for us, but they move up the ladder of emphasis in our lives and may even move to the top of the ladder! Brian Hedrick reminds us of the need for the love of our lives to be our Lord—with all of our heart, soul, mind, and strength.

The wonderful gift of music that God gave us and is encouraged in all of Scripture is one of those "good things" that has the ability to entrap our hearts and become too big of a focus of our hearts. Music has incredible power to communicate, encourage, inspire, and resonate in our entire being. It's not just an aural experience as listener or technical showcase as performer. God gave us this gift as a tool for worshiping him. But God also allows it for teaching and praise. How many of us remember the light and fun Sunday School songs that taught us about God and God's goodness? Music is an amazing gift in so many ways. That includes the music of the great masters with symphonies and choral works.

I have many memories of attending symphony concerts and being moved to tears at the pure beauty of the music and artistry of the performers. When I left the concerts, I literally could not speak or I would have burst into tears of emotion realizing the incredible gifts that were given to the composer and the performers by our great God. I also remember similar experiences in moments of worship through music where I was moved by God's goodness to love us the way he does. Music does have power!

I have served as God's musician for more than forty years, with the focus of my craft being to create musical offerings for worship of our Lord and Savior. I know that God gifted me to do this, but I have never lost sight of the purpose of this music. It is solely to glorify God and not me!

As you read Brian Hedrick's words of direction and encouragement, look at your heart closely. It's not about us; it's all about God.

Camp Kirkland
Professional Arranger and Orchestrator
Music Director, Global Missions Project

Acknowledgments

Even though the initial inspiration for this book may have come from my experiences in secular musical groups, I must acknowledge my profound gratitude to the volunteer instrumentalists of Johnson Ferry Baptist Church, who exemplify for me the ideal attitude toward music, as I serve with them as their director. They utilize the tool of music well, as they lead our congregation in worship every Sunday. I am truly honored to be their director and a fellow servant with them in the house of the Lord.

As far as my acknowledgement to those that assisted me with the writing of this book, I am deeply indebted to Larry D. Ellis, who was a classmate in all three years of my doctoral study at the Robert E. Webber Institute for Worship Studies (IWS). When I first approached Larry about the idea for this book, he responded very enthusiastically, offering me great encouragement to pursue the concept. When I forwarded an early draft to him, he responded almost immediately, with detailed feedback for me that was extremely helpful. He has also been a source of encouragement in potential publishing options, being a published author himself.

In the midst of his busy duties, James Hart, president of IWS, took the time to give me direction on this book, and I am grateful. Jim introduced me to the doctrine of *creatio ex nihilo* (creation out of nothing), which was the missing piece of the puzzle for my opening chapter. When I searched for resources to explain this doctrine, I was delighted to find the perfect source, co-authored by William Lane Craig, who is a friend and member of the church I have served for twenty-six years. He was a helpful resource in my doctoral studies and continues to be a significant influence in the writing of this book.

Robert Myers, general editor for Webber Institute Books, has also been a tremendous source of encouragement in this project, showing great patience as he offered many suggestions to expand the scope of the book.

When I was pursuing my doctorate in worship studies at IWS, Andrew Hill was my thesis supervisor, for which I was extremely grateful, given that he is a respected Old Testament scholar. My gratitude extends to him, as he reviewed an early manuscript of the book and gave me practical, insightful feedback and ideas for crucial content.

I also want to thank Will Fulkerson, a very talented young man, who generously agreed to provide his profound testimony for this book. Because of a medical condition in his hands, Will is unable to type, so he agreed to record his testimony, at my request. He also agreed to read an early version of the book, to better understand how his testimony would fit into the scope of the book. Prior to hearing his story,

I was praying for relevant testimonies to include in this book; his story was the perfect answer to that prayer.

Jana Young graciously agreed to review the manuscript and contribute her perspective on the subject, as a Christian college professor working in a secular music setting. I am grateful for her testimony on how to be light shining in the darkness (Matt. 5:16).

In the final stages of the writing process, Ken Hughes provided firm but thoughtful criticism of the manuscript, challenging me to consider that musicians can be equally devoted to music as to Christ, without making music an idol. Thank you, Kenn, for speaking the truth to me in love.

I would like to thank my wife, Mellonee, for putting up with my obsession with getting this book written. I truly felt God's leading in addressing this issue and although she struggled at times to understand my perspective, I am grateful for her support and encouragement.

Finally, and ultimately, I thank my Lord and Savior Jesus Christ, who is the object of and inspiration for all our worship. To him be glory and honor and blessing, now and forever. Amen.

Introduction

As a lifelong church instrumentalist, I have often participated in community orchestras, in addition to playing regularly in church instrumental groups. I enjoy the beauty and challenge of secular classical music and consider my participation a chance to be a representative for Christ outside the four walls of the church. Since I am a church instrumental director, I welcome the experience of simply being a player-participant in rehearsals and concerts, rather than my usual practice of directing every rehearsal and only playing for worship on Sunday.

As I have played in these community groups over the years, I have noticed an attitude from the musicians toward the higher ideal of music that is strikingly similar to the way we revere Jesus Christ in worship. In the same way that we might say, "It's all about Jesus," I have heard them say with equally great conviction, "It's all about the music."

The more I observed this reverence for music, the more I realized that music had essentially become an idol to many players in the community orchestras in which I participated. One of the fundamental commandments in both Judaism and Christianity is "You shall have no other gods before me" (Exod. 20:3). Only God should occupy the throne as Lord of our lives, but these musicians had effectively taken God off the throne and replaced him with their divine concept of music. In fact, they were willing to sacrifice much for the sake of this idol: long rehearsals and late nights at weekend concerts. They sacrificed family time for the lifestyle required to participate in these groups and committed themselves to hours and hours of practice. As Christians, we are asked to sacrifice much for the sake of the gospel, and the level of sacrifice for these musicians' "god" can be strangely similar.

Music is also conspicuous as an idol in the popular music culture, and it includes idolization of the musicians who perform music. This is evident by the sheer number of television shows, beginning with *American Idol*, that exalt the talents of the next great musician and singer. These shows include *America's Got Talent*, *The Voice*, *Britain's Got Talent*, and *The X Factor*, among others. In the established music industry, popular musicians have cult-like followings from their fans, and many of them encourage this passionate and irrational devotion, which smacks of idolatry.

Perhaps the most disturbing part of this musical idolatry is realizing that the same mindset can occur inside the church. We live in an era where worship leaders are often hired based on their musical qualifications, with no compelling consideration for their spiritual walk and Christian testimony. Many times these staff members, whose role is to guide others in worship, are considered solely on their musical experience and expertise. Such factors are important but should not be relied upon as the only determinants in their qualifications. Musical background and skill level, in these cases, have superseded all other job qualifications, signaling an alarming imbalance in essential church priorities. This observation is confirmed by Daniel I. Block: "Ministers of music are hired for their musical skill, achievements, creativity, or enthusiasm on stage, without sufficient concern for their knowledge of Scripture, their orthodoxy, or their theology of worship."[1]

Another area where this misplaced devotion is evident is in the Praise and Worship Movement, where music is often viewed as synonymous with Christian worship, ignoring the historical prescription in worship, established over the centuries, of the priority of Word and Table. I have heard stories of two- to three-hour worship services, with only a fifteen-minute devotional from the pastor and no observance of the Lord's Supper. Everything else in the service focused exclusively on the music. Of course, music can be a great expression of worship, but services such as these are extremely out of balance in the full expression of biblical worship.

Equally disturbing is the phenomenon of Christians choosing churches to attend, based on the reputation of the music or the musicians leading worship: "They have great worship" (synonymous with music) or "they have a great worship band." This factor often seems to be often more important in their church choice than the sound biblical teaching of the pastor, the quality of the fellowship, the devotion of the congregation to Christ, or the outreach ministry of the church. In the words of Block, "Delighted—if not intoxicated—by the crowds, we may be oblivious to the reality that a packed house may be proof of disingenuous (calculated) worship rather than the worship acceptable to God."[2]

Sharperiron.org, a website hosted by people of historic fundamentalist conviction (based on Prov. 27:17—"Iron sharpens iron, so one man sharpens another"), conducted a survey in March 2014, asking the question, "Do you think music has become an idol in our churches?"[3] The survey sample was relatively small (only 24 individuals), but the results still support the concern in this area:

Yes, in most churches	33% (8 votes)
Yes, in many but not most churches	38% (9 votes)
Yes, in some instances but not commonly	17% (4 votes)
Unsure	8% (2 votes)
No	4% (1 vote)

After an exhaustive search for surveys related to this topic, this solitary and modest poll was all my search uncovered—which reflects a relative lack of concern for this important issue in our culture.

W. David O. Taylor affirms that "The possibility for misuse and abuse of the arts [music] in worship remains a constant danger for churches in all traditions and contexts. This includes, for instance, the possibility of idolatry (confusing Creator and creature)."[4] Consider Paul's words in his letter to the Romans: "They exchanged the truth about God for a lie, and worshiped and served created things rather than the Creator—who is forever praised. Amen" (Rom. 1:25, NIV).

Please note that this book is not an indictment against intensely devoted Christian musicians, who are passionate in their devotion to Christ, while being equally passionate about their music. My main concern is with individuals, both inside and outside the Christian faith, who have displaced devotion to God with devotion to music.

I should mention that this book is written mostly from a Western music perspective. The standard music history textbook used while I was in college, Donald Jay Grout's *A History of Western Music,* identifies Western music as "the musical system of western Europe and the Americas" and "is but one of several among the civilizations of the world."[5] Music from ancient Judaism and early Christianity is also considered in chapter 2, but the perspective of the book as a whole is decidedly Western.

I humbly offer this book for the reader's consideration, in the interest of greater awareness of music idolatry that often goes unnoticed by most individuals and with the goal of emphasizing the proper practice of honoring God in the expression of worship. We urgently need to put music back in its proper perspective and rightful place, both inside and outside the church. I love music and have loved it since I was a child. In fact, I have devoted my life to music, both as a music educator and a church musician. But it is not the driving force in my life as a believer in Jesus Christ. There is only one occupant on the throne of my life, and it is not music. To God alone be the glory (*Soli Deo Gloria*)!

NOTES

[1]Daniel I. Block, *For the Glory of God: Recovering a Biblical Theology of Worship* (Grand Rapids: Baker Academic, 2014), 236.

[2]Ibid.

[3]Ed Vasicek, "Do you think music has become an idol in our churches?," March 26, 2014, https://sharperiron.org/forum/poll-do-you-think-music-has-become-idol-our-churches (accessed Nov. 1, 2019).

[4]W. David O. Taylor, *Glimpses of the New Creation: Worship and the Formative Power of the Arts* (Grand Rapids: Eerdmans Publishing Co., 2019), 245.

[5]Donald Jay Grout, *A History of Western Music,* rev. ed. (New York: W.W. Norton and Co., 1960), xi.

Chapter 1

Music as a Creation of God

So who created music anyway? This question is a mystery and cannot be definitively determined. Iain Morley's book on the prehistory of music explores the origins of music, but his conclusion includes this concession from David Huron: "Most scholars have wisely steered clear of the issue of music origins, since clearly the enterprise is patently speculative. At its worst, proposals concerning music's origin are fiction masquerading as scholarship."[1] There simply are no verifiable records of early human experience with music, making any theories purely guesswork.

Charles Darwin observed that man's ability to make music is "among the most mysterious with which he is endowed," since "neither the enjoyment nor the capacity of producing musical notes are faculties of the least use to man in reference to his daily habits of life."[2] When considering the probable origins of music in prehistoric man, Jeremy Montagu maintains that "music in its earliest form must surely have preceded speech. The ability to produce something melodic, a murmuration of sound, something between humming and crooning to a baby, must have long preceded the ability to form consonants and vowels that are essential constituents of speech."[3] Gary Tomlinson agrees with this "close relation of the origins of musicking and language."[4] He says there are basically two camps in the relationship between language development and the development of music making: "Sometimes language has been seen to give rise to music, as an outgrowth or aftereffect; much more often musicking has been understood as a kind of Ur-language (basic or original language) of emotion, resulting only later in rational, propositional language."[5]

So both Montagu and Tomlinson believe it is more likely that music predated speech, although Tomlinson admits that "The question is pressing for musicking since, whatever else it is, it is an evanescent act or set of acts that fades as it sounds. Its product does not have the staying power of mammoths painted on cave walls or the heft of carved 'Venus' figurines."[6]

Israeli musicologist Joachim Braun takes a different perspective on the earliest musical expression. Based on the comparative method, which is studying more contemporary primitive civilizations, he believes that the earliest music may have been percussive in nature:

> In lieu of musical instruments in the strict sense, people probably used various objects, both natural and man-made, including tools and even their own bodies, to produce music.
>
> This assumption is plausible enough considering the basic forms of music-making or even noise-production familiar even today from many parts of the world, including the clapping of hands, stamping of feet, beating on one's chest, or slapping one's thigh. As effective as such activity is for producing primitive rhythms, it still leaves behind no tangible material witness. Hence the comparative method offers us the best hypothesis to date for describing the beginnings of music production.[7]

Braun differs from Morley and Tomlinson in their view of the earliest likely expression of music (vocal and melodic vs. percussive and rhythmic), but they all agree that due to the lack of "tangible material witness,"[8] any theories advanced are purely speculative. We simply cannot be sure what man's earliest expression of music might have been.

From a biblical perspective, the first mention of music in Scripture occurs in Genesis 4, as the writer goes through the descendants of Cain, who at the time in the account, was the sole surviving son of the first man, Adam: "Adah gave birth to Jabal; he was the father of those who dwell in tents and have livestock. His brother's name was Jubal; he was the father of all those who play the lyre and pipe" (vv. 20-21).

According to this account, Jubal was the seventh generation after Adam. Even though there is no way to determine an exact date, this evidence still confirms that music was a part of early man's experience, based on the biblical record.

It is important to acknowledge the apparent similarities, as we study early forms of music across cultures. According to Morley, "It would appear that musical behaviors amongst humans involve the encoding of sounds into pitches (usually between three and seven) which are unequally separated across the scale, including the perfect fifth, favoring consonance and harmony over dissonance, and organizing sequences of sounds so that they have a temporal relationship to each other."[9] In other words, there are basic principles of music that are constant, even over vastly different cultures and people groups. It is as if these principles, or building blocks of music, were already in place before humans even began the practice of music making. I propose that this idea demonstrates that music was not created by humans, but *discovered.* Ultimately, God is the creator of music. Music is a creation.

The Bible suggests that music predates humanity. In the Old Testament book of Job, when "the Lord answered Job out of the whirlwind" (38:1), God challenged Job to consider the implications of God's creative power:

> Where were you when I laid the foundations of the earth?
> Tell me, if you have understanding,
> Who set its measurements? Since you know.
> Or who stretched the line on it?
> On what were its bases sunk?
> Or who laid its cornerstone,
> *When the morning stars sang together*
> And all the sons of God shouted for joy?
> (38:4-7, emphasis mine)

Verse 7, saying that "the morning stars sang together" at creation, suggests that music preceded even humankind's creation. What is mentioned in the passage above is descriptive of the events of the first four days of creation (Gen. 1:3-19). Man and woman were not created until day six (vv. 26-28), after the singing of the morning stars.

In spite of the speculation about music's origin, one critical Christian doctrine must be factored into the equation: the doctrine of *creatio ex nihilo*, or creation out of nothing. According to Paul Copan and William Lane Craig, this doctrine means that "Without God's initiating creation, only God exists. Upon creation, we have a universe because God willed it into finite, temporal being. Thus, creation out of nothing affirms that the universe is contingent on God, not just in having its (continued) existence in being ... but also in having its temporal origination from nothing preexistent, but simply by the will and word of God."[10]

The biblical support for this doctrine comes from both the Old and New Testaments, beginning with Genesis 1:1, "In the beginning God created the heavens and the earth." The phrase "heavens and the earth" is a merism, which is the use of two contrasting words to refer to an entirety. Copan and Craig confirm that "there is 'no single word in the Hebrew language' to express totality; thus, this phrase is used."[11] "The expression 'the heavens and the earth' refers to absolutely everything... All things had a beginning, and God is their originator."[12]

Several passages from the book of Psalms also affirm the origination of the "heavens and earth" (absolutely everything) in God and God alone, including these three passages:

> How blessed is he whose help is the God of Jacob,
> Whose hope is in the Lord his God,
> Who made *heaven and earth*,
> The sea and all that is in them;
> Who keeps faith forever.
> (146:5-6, emphasis mine)

> Of old You founded *the earth*,
> And *the heavens* are the work of Your hands.
> Even they will perish, but You endure;
> And all of them will wear out like a garment;
> Like clothing You will change them and they will be changed.
> But You are the same,
> And Your years will not come to an end.
> (102:25-27, emphasis mine)

> Before the mountains were born
> Or You gave birth to the earth and the world,
> Even from everlasting to everlasting, You are God.
> (90:2)

Throughout the Old Testament, in passages such as these, we realize that God is the Supreme Initiator. God speaks and all things come into being. The New Testament is equally replete with passages that support the doctrine of *creatio ex nihilo*:

> All things came into being through Him, and apart from Him nothing came into being that has come into being. (John 1:3)

> ... God, who gives life to the dead and calls into being that which does not exist. (Rom. 4:17b)

> By faith we understand that the worlds were prepared by the word of God, so that what is seen was not made out of things which are visible. (Heb. 11:3)

> For from Him and through Him and to Him are all things. (Rom. 11:36a)

> For by Him all things were created, both in the heavens and on earth, visible and invisible, whether thrones or dominions or rulers or authorities—all things have been created through Him and for Him. (Col. 1:16)

> Yet for us there is but one God, the Father, from whom are all things and we exist for Him; and one Lord, Jesus Christ, by whom are all things, and we exist through Him. (1 Cor. 8:6)

In both the Old and New Testaments, God is sovereign over all and everything is contingent on God for its being. All that exists apart from God is creation and originates from God's action as Creator. Copan and Craig conclude: "So the only meaningful distinction between beings is 'Creator' and 'creation.' There is nothing in between."[13]

Thomas J. Terry and J. Ryan Lister maintain that our ability to create (i.e. to make music) is derivative: "Only God's creation is *ex nihilo* (out of nothing), which means our creativity is never purely our own; it relies on our Creator and builds out of His creation. As His image bearers—created by God to be like Him—our creativity *reflects* His."[14] We create because God created us. We are created in God's image, and part of that image involves the ability to be creative creatures. Our creative gifts are ultimately not our own and therefore should be used in gratitude to God and for God's glory. Otherwise, music and other expressions of creativity can become idols, the very idea I am confronting with this book.

Music then, as a creation of God, when worshiped and served in place of God, is a perfect example of what the Apostle Paul describes in his letter to the Romans (the theme text for this book): "They exchanged the truth about God for a lie, and worshiped and served created things rather than the Creator—who is forever praised. Amen" (Rom. 1:25, NIV).

F.F. Bruce explains what is meant by this verse: "By 'the lie' is apparently meant the denial of the fundamental truth that God is God; it is the rejection of his self-revelation as Creator and Savior, righteous and merciful Judge of all, which leads to worship due to him alone being offered to another."[15] Music is a creation of God, especially created for God's praise. To make it the object of our praise, either inside or outside the church, is to "exchange the truth about God for a lie."

If, as Colossians 1:16 proclaims, "all things have been created through Him and for Him," then all of creation's sounds worship God, as W. David O. Taylor points out: "If all of creation's sounds worship God, precisely by fulfilling their created purpose, then humanity's calling is to give particular voice to creation's sonic praise and to do so in all sorts of ways, for all sorts of reasons, and in all sorts of contexts. In the context of corporate worship, the musical arts can be enlisted to serve specific activities and purposes in a wide range of ways, and the Triune God would not have it otherwise."[16]

In summary, God is the creator of all things, including music. Even though music's origins cannot be definitely determined, the principles of music are constant over vastly different cultures, therefore attesting to music as God's creation and humankind's discovery. This is reinforced by the doctrine of *creatio ex nihilo,* which establishes that God created everything out of nothing. With music proven then as a creation and God as the Creator, music as an idol is a perfect example of worshiping the created thing, rather than the Creator.

The original, foundational ideal of music created for and used for God's glory was the prevailing practice in biblical history, in both ancient Judaism and early Christianity. We will explore the roots of proper historical musical practice in the next chapter.

NOTES

[1]Iain Morley, *The Prehistory of Music: Human Evolution, Archaeology, and the Origins of Musicality* (Oxford: Oxford University Press, 2013), 307.

[2]Ibid., 1.

[3]Jeremy Montagu, "How Music and Instruments Began: A Brief Overview of the Origin and Entire Development of Music, from Its Earliest Stages" in *Frontiers in Sociology* 2:8 (doi: 103389/fsoc.2017.00008, 2017), 3.

[4]Gary Tomlinson, *A Million Years of Music: The Emergence of Human Modernity* (Brooklyn, NY: Zone Books, 2015), 11.

[5]Ibid.

[6]Ibid., 12.

[7]Joachim Braun, *Music in Ancient Israel/Palestine: Archaeological, Written, and Comparative Sources* (Grand Rapids: Eerdmans Publishing co., 2002), 47.

[8]Ibid.

[9]Morley, *The Prehistory of Music,* 7.

[10]Paul Copan and William Lane Craig, *Creation Out of Nothing: A Biblical, Philosophical, and Scientific Exploration* (Grand Rapids: Baker Academic, 2004), 15.

[11]Ibid., 59.

[12]Ibid., 65.

[13]Ibid., 15.

[14]Thomas J. Terry and J. Ryan Lister, *Images and Idols: Creativity for the Christian Life* (Chicago: Moody Publishers, 2018), 50.

[15]F.F. Bruce, *1 and 2 Thessalonians,* vol. 45, *Word Biblical Commentary* (Nashville: Thomas Nelson, 1982), 174.

[16]W. David O. Taylor, *Glimpses of the New Creation: Worship and the Formative Power of the Arts* (Grand Rapids: Eerdmans Publishing Co., 2019), 79.

Chapter 2

Music, Created for God's Glory

Examining the table of contents in Donald Grout's *A History of Western Music*, which gives us a definitive outline of Western music history, we see that the first three chapters are dominated by sections referencing sacred music: The Early Christian Church, Gregorian Chant and the Roman Liturgy, Types of Gregorian Chant, and Notre Dame Organum.[1] In the conclusion of chapter 3, Grout makes this statement: "At the beginning of the thirteenth century practically all polyphonic (multi-voiced) music was sacred; by the end of the century, although there was yet no clear distinction between sacred and secular musical styles, polyphonic settings were being written for both sacred and secular texts."[2] Grout thus establishes AD 1300, more or less, as a dividing point between the predominance of sacred music and the emergence of secular forms of music in Western history.

Later, in Grout's table of contents, sacred designations dominate again, in chapters 8–13, with multiple references to the Reformation and church music. There is also mention of the music of Johann Sebastian Bach and George Frédéric Handel,[3] who both devoted much of their musical efforts to church and sacred music. After chapter 13, there are no further sections that can be interpreted as referencing sacred music, basically after the classical period (roughly between 1730 and 1820). This absence is due primarily to the advent of the Enlightenment, "a mainly 18th-cent. European philosophical movement characterized by a reliance on reason and experience rather than dogma and tradition."[4] Also known as the Age of Reason, the Enlightenment challenged almost all forms of authority, including organized religion and the church. The influence of the movement continues today and has contributed to an increasingly secular society.

Throughout Western history, we observe the obvious predominant influence of sacred music (music written for and expressed through the church) in early historical practice. With the introduction of secular forms in the early thirteenth century, the popularity of sacred music gradually diminished due to the increasing development of secular music, which became dominant in the late classical period.

With this broad overview of music history in mind, I now examine specific foundational periods and influential composers in music history, which demonstrate and establish the practice of music, created for the glory of God.

Music in Ancient Judaism

Music in ancient Judaism was an important element of both temple and synagogue worship. Judaism also profoundly influenced early Christian worship. Church musicologist Donald P. Hustad provides this summary: "Through almost three thousand years of Hebrew/Christian history, music has been inseparable from worship, and the Bible contains much of our early heritage of worship song. The Psalms come from many periods of the ancient Jewish culture, and they were augmented by canticles that date back to Israel's deliverance from Egypt."[5]

The Psalms, also known as the ancient hymnbook of Israel, were written to be sung in praise to Almighty God, and occupied much of the formal liturgy of ancient Judaism. According to Sigmund Mowinckel, psalms are not mere poetry: "they are real cult [a system of religious worship or ritual] psalms composed for and used in the actual services in the Temple."[6]

It is interesting to note that before the time of King David, Israel's worship was mostly silent, lacking music. Once David ascended the throne as king, there was a sudden explosion of musical expression.[7] The Levites (men from the tribe of Levi), whose job was to transport the Tabernacle through the wilderness, found themselves without a job when David, under God's direction, established Jerusalem as the permanent site for Israel's worship.[8] David then set the Levites apart as musicians and servants in the sanctuary (1 Chron. 15:16), which eventually became the Temple, built by his son, Solomon. In the dedication service for the Temple, there were 120 priests alone blowing trumpets, among many other Levites playing cymbals, harps and lyres, accompanying the levitical choir in praise of God (2 Chron. 5:11-12). These large numbers of Levite musicians illustrate that employing music to glorify God was a high priority in the worship practices of ancient Judaism, particularly under the reign and influence of King David.

Music in Early Christianity

Temple and synagogue practice influenced worship in early Christianity, which included music as an important element of the worship of the early Christian church. The early church was a singing church, and we see evidence of that practice in the New Testament as the believer's response to Jesus Christ. These musical responses in Scripture have become fixtures in the worship of Christian churches. Hustad explains: "Most of the New Testament songs or hymns have found their way into the enduring liturgy of the church, including the *Magnificat* (Luke 1:46-55), the *Benedictus* (Luke 1:67-79), the *Gloria* (Luke 2:14), and the *Nunc Dimittis* (Luke 2:29-32). New Testament music in worship included psalmody, hymns composed in the church, and spiritual songs—alleluias and songs of jubilation or ecstatic nature."[9]

Even though the New Testament includes many forms and references to music and singing, the music in early Christian worship was not as grand as the music in Israel's Temple worship. This disparity was primarily due to the persecution of early Christians and the clandestine nature of their gatherings for worship and prayer. Early believers were often in danger of being martyred for their faith and worship practices, so they were generally not singing loudly, and definitely not with the accompaniment of trumpets and loud cymbals. Rather, they were most likely quietly singing, with no accompaniment, in a secure and secluded location, so as not to draw attention to themselves. This was the predominant practice through the first three centuries of the church's existence.

The reign of the Roman emperor Constantine triggered a significant change in the visibility and style of Christian worship. When Constantine decreed in AD 313 that Christianity should be tolerated throughout the Roman Empire, Christian worship no longer needed to be practiced in secret. Worship in private homes and underground catacombs (burial places) eventually gave way to worship in elaborate basilicas, built and sanctioned by the Roman Empire. Constantine even converted many pagan temples to buildings for Christian worship. The use of dedicated worship space also affected the expression of music in worship, as it became more elaborate and complex. These developments eventually led to the establishment of the Roman Catholic mass, which focused primarily on the Eucharist (Communion or the Lord's Supper). Church historian James F. White refers to the Eucharist as "the most common form of public worship"[10] for the people, but it eventually resulted in the clergy actively participating in worship and the people simply watching:

> For the lay person attending mass faithfully every Sunday and holy day, the trajectory of this whole period was that of mass becoming more and more remote. A good example of this was the altar-table itself receding further and further from view until it finally became lodged firmly against the east wall of the church. The bishop or priest who formerly had faced the people across the altar-table now turned his back on them… Other instances of progressive remoteness include the disinclination to receive from the chalice which became common in the twelfth century for fear of spilling the blood of Christ.[11]

The Protestant Reformation was a reaction to these distortions of the Roman Catholic Church in worship. Those abuses included the neglect of the public reading and preaching of the Word, the absence of worship in the language of the people (it was universally only in Latin), the observance of the Lord's Supper as the activity of the clergy alone (with the congregation as spectators), and the celebration of the mass being regarded as an offering of the actual physical blood and body of Jesus Christ (with little remembrance of his resurrection and second coming). The reformers addressed these issues with an increased emphasis on reading and preaching the Word in worship, worship in the language of the people, and an increase in participatory worship, specifically congregational singing. James White writes, "If the Reformation period saw an explosion in preaching, it was no less dramatic in the increase in music, particularly as regards congregational singing."[12]

The use of hymnody greatly accelerated during the Reformation, including Martin Luther, who is credited with writing about thirty-seven hymns.[13] It also involved a renewed practice of singing psalms in worship, as encouraged by the reformer, John Calvin. By the end of the seventeenth century and into the eighteenth century, Protestant hymnody was well established, through the efforts of great hymn writers such as Isaac Watts (1674–1748) and the Wesley brothers, John (1703–1791) and Charles (1707–1788). Charles Wesley alone wrote more than 6,500 hymns, many of which are still popular today.

Soli Deo Gloria—the Music of Johann Sebastian Bach

Johann Sebastian Bach (1685–1750) has been acclaimed throughout history as the consummate Christian composer. Patrick Kavanaugh identifies Bach as "almost a kind of 'patron saint' for church musicians."[14] According to R.W.S. Mendl, "No man has ever dedicated his art to God more completely and more consistently than Bach."[15]

Bach spent most of his life as a church musician in Germany, primarily known by his contemporaries as an organist, but he had no concept of his greatness as a "creator" of music.[16] Even though Bach was one of the most prolific composers of all time, only ten of his original compositions were published during his lifetime.[17] Grout notes, "Doubtless he would have been astonished if he had been told that two hundred years after his death his music would be performed and studied everywhere and his name more deeply venerated by musicians than of any other composer."[18]

Bach was greatly influenced by the reforms of Martin Luther, introduced in the two centuries prior to his life. Kavanaugh proclaims him as "the reformer's greatest musical disciple."[19] Interestingly, Bach made no distinctions between his sacred and secular works. They were all written and performed for God's glory. He often inscribed one of the following designations at the beginning or end of his compositions, both sacred and secular:

J. J. (Jesu, juva)—Jesus, aid
I. N. J. (in nomine Jesu)—in the name of Jesus
S. D. G. (soli Deo gloria)—to God alone be glory[20]

The third inscription, *soli Deo gloria,* is the one that truly reflects the theme of Bach's life. As a disciple of Martin Luther and a sincere Lutheran churchman, Kavanaugh maintains that "Bach resoundingly echoed the convictions of Luther, claiming that 'Music's only purpose should be for the glory of God and the recreation of the human spirit.'"[21]

George Frédéric Handel and *Messiah*

Johann Sebastian Bach stands head and shoulders above other composers with his devotion to creating music for the glory of God, but he does not stand alone. His contemporary, George Frédéric Handel (1685–1759), composed one of the most inspiring choral works of all time. His oratorio, *Messiah,* was commissioned by a Dublin charity for a benefit performance in 1741, and used a libretto given to him by a wealthy friend that was based on the life of Christ and taken entirely from the Bible.[22] This friend, Charles Jennens, was devoted to Handel's music, helping finance much of the publishing of his musical works. The scriptural text of the *Messiah* libretto, compiled by Jennens, came from the King James Bible and from the Cloverdale Psalter, the version of the Psalms included with the Book of Common Prayer.

What is most amazing about the creation of this profound work is the relatively short time it took for Handel to complete it: all 260 pages of manuscript in a mere twenty-four days! It is said that he was "so absorbed with the work that he rarely left his room, hardly stopping to eat."[23] Composing *Messiah* proved to be a profoundly emotional experience for him and later, "as he groped for words to describe what he experienced, he quoted St. Paul (2 Cor. 12:2), saying, 'Whether I was in the body or out of my body when I wrote it I know not.'"[24] This quote, used by Paul to describe a vision from God, implies that Handel felt he was guided by the hand of God through the incredible spiritual experience of composing the musical score.

Handel personally conducted more than thirty performances of *Messiah* before his death in 1759, but the impact of his work continues to this day. Robert Manson Myers, in his book, *Handel's Messiah,* says it "has probably done more to convince thousands of mankind that there is a God about us than all the theological works ever written."[25] Personally, I have experienced the profound impact of this work, as it was performed every year at the seminary I attended (Southwestern Baptist Theological Seminary in Ft. Worth, Texas), and the entire full score was the required literature for our graduate conducting classes, including the overture, pastorale and all choruses, arias and recitatives.

Messiah was not the only sacred work Handel composed. His voluminous listing of compositions includes fourteen sacred oratorios besides *Messiah* and fifty-seven sacred vocal works. Handel's devotion to Christ extended through his music and into his personal life. He was described as "a devout follower of Christ and widely known for his concern for others."[26]

Anton Bruckner and Sacred Music

After the Baroque period and progressing through the classical period, music became increasingly secular. One exception to the dominance of secular music following the classical period was the music of Anton Bruckner (1824–1896). Grout identifies Bruckner as "the most important church composer of the later nineteenth century" and describes him as "a solitary, simple, profoundly religious soul."[27] Trained in music at a monastery, Bruckner was a virtuoso on the organ and a lifelong composer of sacred music. "Bruckner succeeded as no one before him in uniting the spiritual and technical resources of the nineteenth century symphony with a reverent and liturgical approach to the sacred texts."[28]

When Bruckner encountered early criticism of his music, he persevered. Kavanaugh explains that believing his talent was a trust given by God, "he once explained with deep emotion, 'They want me to write in a different way. I could, but I must not. Out of thousands I was given this talent by God, only I. Sometime I will have to give an account of myself. How would the Father in Heaven judge me if I followed others and not Him?'"[29] Over a life of success and failures, Anton Bruckner's steadfast faith was the one constant. According to biographer Hans Ferdinand Redlick, Bruckner was perhaps the only composer of his century whose entire musical output was determined by his religious faith.[30] Even though Bruckner is best known for his eleven symphonies, his commitment to his religious faith is exemplified by the sheer number of religious works he composed (fifty-nine total), including seven masses, two requiems, one religious cantata, five psalm settings, one *Te Deum* hymn, and one *Magnificat* hymn.

Many other composers have had profoundly spiritual lives, as evidenced by the number of biographies listed in the table of contents of Patrick Kavanaugh's *The Spiritual Lives of the Great Composers*. The list includes composers from the time of Bach and Handel (the Baroque Period), but also composers from the Classical, Romantic, and Twentieth Century periods of music. This consistency demonstrates that the practice of writing music for the glory of God was established early and often, and continues on in a consistent basis throughout history. Though I'm asserting that music can become an idol, the original design was intended as a creation of

God, created for God's glory. Bach, Handel, Bruckner, and others were champions in their commitment to that original and true ideal.

There is a well-established precedent throughout history, beginning in biblical times, of music created for God's glory. This music was a reflection of what Brennan S. McPherson calls "an eternal Music that brought light and form to the universe."[31] Sacred music dominated musical literature through the early thirteenth century. Even beyond that there are excellent examples of music written for God's glory, including the *Soli Deo Gloria* ideal of Johann Sebastian Bach, the unprecedented phenomenon of George Frédéric Handel and his masterpiece, *Messiah,* and the tremendous output of sacred music by Anton Bruckner.

In the next chapter I will explore the potential of music to become an idol, despite God's original intention in its creation.

NOTES

[1]Donald Jay Grout, *A History of Western Music,* rev. ed. (New York: W.W. Norton and Co., Inc., 1960), vii.

[2]Ibid., 114-115.

[3]Ibid., viii.

[4]*Webster's New World College Dictionary,* 4th ed., s.v. "the Enlightenment."

[5]Donald P. Hustad, "Music in the Worship of the Old Testament," in *Music and the Arts in Christian Worship,* ed. Robert E. Webber, vol. 4, book 1, *The Complete Library of Christian Worship* (Nashville: Star Song, 1994), 188.

[6]Sigmund Mowinckel, *The Psalms in Israel's Worship* (Grand Rapids: Eerdmans Publishing Co., 2004), xliii.

[7]For more on this, see Peter J. Leithart, *From Silence to Song: The Davidic Liturgical Revolution* (Moscow, ID: Canon Press, 2003).

[8]Brian L. Hedrick, *The Biblical Foundations of Instrumental Music in Worship: Four Pillars* (Denver, CO: Outskirts Press, 2009), 29.

[9]Donald P. Hustad, "Music in the Worship of the New Testament," in *Music and the Arts in Christian Worship,* ed. Robert E. Webber, vol. 4, book 1, *The Complete Library of Christian Worship* (Nashville: Star Song, 1994), 192.

[10]James F. White, *A Brief History of Christian Worship* (Nashville: Abingdon Press, 1993), 86.

[11]Ibid., 88, 90.

[12]White, 136.

[13]Ibid., 137.

[14]Patrick Kavanaugh, *Spiritual Lives of the Great Composers,* rev. (Grand Rapids: Zondervan, 1996), 18.

[15]RWS Mendl, *The Divine Quest in Music* (London: Rockliff Publishing Corporation, 1957), 57.

[16]Ibid.

[17]Kavanaugh, *Spiritual Lives of the Great Composers,* 19.

[18]Grout, *A History of Western Music,* 417.

[19]Kavanaugh, *Spiritual Lives of the Great Composers,* 19.

[20]Grout, *A History of Western Music,* 421.

[21]Kavanaugh, *Spiritual Lives of the Great Composers,* 19.

[22]Ibid., 29.

[23]Ibid., 30.

[24]Ibid.

[25]Robert Manson Myers, *Handel's Messiah: A Touchstone of Taste* (New York: Octagon Books, 1971), 238.

[26]Kavanaugh, *Spiritual Lives of the Great Composers*, 31, quoting William Coxe, *Anecdotes of George Frideric Handel and John Christopher Smith* (London: Bulmer, 1799), 29.

[27]Grout, *A History of Western Music*, 556.

[28]Ibid.

[29]Kavanaugh, *Spiritual Lives of the Great Composers*, 133-134.

[30]Hans Ferdinand Redlick, *Bruckner and Mahler* (London: J.M. Dent Ltd., 1955), 37.

[31]Brennan S. McPherson, *Flood: The Story of Noah and the Family Who Raised Him* (Sparta, WI: McPherson Publishing, 2017), 1.

Chapter 3

Music as an Idol of Man

Webster's Dictionary defines an idol as "an image of a god, used as an object or instrument of worship." An alternate definition provided is "any object of ardent or excessive devotion or admiration." Obviously, the first definition is the one most people equate with the word idol and cannot be applied to music. The second definition certainly can. In fact, in our modern world, graven images are seldom seen, but idols that match the second definition are widespread. Idolatry of this sort is rampant, as devotion to God gives way to devotion to career, family, wealth, hobbies, fitness, sports, politics, and causes. Allen P. Ross comments:

> The modern world, at least in the West, is not plagued by a vast array of idols as was the ancient Near East. But the spirit of idolatry remains, for anything that rivals God in his rightful place as Sovereign Lord is a violation of the first principle of the faith.[1] It does not matter if the object is Baal, or science, or money. If it robs God of his proper glory, then it diminishes any devotion offered to him.[2]

Timothy Keller points out that even though we may not physically kneel before a statue of a god, our idolatry can take many other forms that are just as serious, including devotion to body image through fitness and exercise, or money and career to gain wealth and prestige.[3] Keller adds, "The Bible makes it clear that we cannot confine idolatry to literal bowing down before the images of false gods. It can be done internally in the soul and heart without being done externally and literally."[4] Musicologist Harold M. Best applies this concept to music: "There is really no difference between someone carving a god out of what is otherwise a piece of firewood and someone else who happens upon or makes a certain kind of music, expecting it to govern the actions of those hearing it and using it."[5] In those cases, the thing created—music—then becomes something abhorrent to God, an idol.

This exaltation of music and its power to control can create such a huge influence on a devoted life that it can become the central focus and motivation for living. Best explains further and warns, "As artists and music makers, we must avoid the assumption that something made can be allowed to switch its role from handiwork *under* dominion to handiwork *having* dominion, assuming prerogatives it does not inherently possess."[6] To fall under this error is to "worship and serve created things rather than the Creator" (Rom. 1:25).

The Bible is full of passages about idolatry, which was the foundational sin in the Old Testament and extending into the New Testament period. The first appendix to this book (see p. 79) references the overwhelming number of those Scripture passages, specifically targeting denunciations against idolatry and passages exposing the folly of idolatry. Of all these references, one of the most insightful and graphic is Isaiah 44:9-20, which exposes the folly of idolatry and its insidious prevalence:

> Those who fashion a graven image are all of them futile, and their precious things are of no profit; even their own witnesses fail to see or know, so that they will be put to shame. Who has fashioned a god or cast an idol to no profit? Behold, all his companions will be put to shame, for the craftsmen themselves are mere men. Let them all assemble themselves, let them stand up, let them tremble, let them together be put to shame.
>
> The man shapes iron into a cutting tool and does his work over the coals, fashioning it with hammers and working it with his strong arm. He also gets hungry and his strength fails; he drinks no water and becomes weary. *Another* shapes wood, he extends a measuring line; he outlines it with red chalk. He works it with planes and outlines it with a compass, and makes it like the form of a man, like the beauty of man, so that it may sit in a house. Surely he cuts cedars for himself, and takes a cypress or an oak and raises *it* for himself among the trees of the forest. He plants a fir, and the rain makes it grow. Then it becomes *something* for a man to burn, so he takes one of them and warms himself; he also makes a fire to bake bread. He also makes a god and worships it; he makes it a graven image and falls down before it. Half of it he burns in the fire; over *this* half he eats meat as he roasts a roast and is satisfied. He also warms himself and says, "Aha! I am warm, I have seen the fire." But the rest of it he makes into a god, his graven image. He falls down before it and worships; he also prays to it and says, "Deliver me, for you are my god."
>
> They do not know, nor do they understand, for He has smeared over their eyes so that they cannot see and their hearts so that they cannot comprehend. No one recalls, nor is there knowledge or understanding to say, "I have burned half of it in the fire and also have baked bread over its coals. I roast meat and eat *it*. Then I make the rest of it into an abomination, I fall down before a block of wood!" He feeds on ashes; a deceived heart has turned him aside. And he cannot deliver himself, nor say, "Is there not a lie in my right hand?"

Best points out two broad points that Isaiah is making in this passage "that go beyond the obvious and into the heart of our common condition: (1) Idolatry is the act of shaping something that we allow to shape us. (2) We are (therefore) blinded by a simple contradiction: what we serve is made out of the same stuff that in other circumstances serves us."[7] Isaiah's words in this passage of Scripture are a rejection of all human attempts to fabricate gods based on our own imagination.

With these concepts of idolatry in mind, it is not hard to imagine music as an idol in the lives of many musicians and even non-musicians. It has tremendous appeal as an object of excessive devotion. Individuals can become so obsessed with musical pursuits that they neglect family and community, and though we don't literally see them bowing down to music, it is the object of supreme reverence in their heart and soul. Evidence of this obsession can be seen in things that are generally good things but suggest an imbalanced life. School chorus, band, and orchestra programs have hundreds of students involved, but many of these students ignore their more academic studies, because they only care about making music. Consider the testimony of jazz saxophonist Con Campbell:

> In my final two years of high school, I basically ignored all my other studies. I practiced saxophone four hours a day—during the school day and at night. While my fellow school students were hitting the books to get into the university courses they wanted, I played saxophone. Scales, tunes, long notes, reeds, listening, transcribing, and gigs were my life. Nothing else mattered.[8]

In addition to neglecting their academic studies, young people sometimes drop out of school to pursue their musical dream of becoming a star, often with the unreserved support of family and friends. If they do stay in school, they often go to colleges around the country that are inundated with optimistic music majors, many more than the music industry and school music programs can support. The result is that many of these individuals are eventually forced to resort to other careers to make a living, thereby abandoning their dream.

But it is not only these tangible evidences of music's power in the human life that factor into the temptation to idolatry. There is also something intangible, a powerful draw to music that is difficult to define. The allure that comes from music making is often labeled as something spiritual. This mystical quality of music can blur the line between devotion to God and devotion to music, especially in the church. Outside of the church, though, the spiritual attraction of music can easily and unconsciously take the place of God.

As a classically trained musician, one of my favorite composers is Gustav Mahler. Of all the playlists I have heard while streaming music, the one I listen to the most is the Mahler symphonies. I played in various community orchestras for years before I finally had the chance to experience the thrill of playing Mahler's music. When the Georgia Symphony Orchestra announced an upcoming program of his *Symphony No. 5*, naturally all the musicians in the orchestra were very excited. I considered it the opportunity of my lifetime, and I probably devoted more time to preparing for the first rehearsal on that piece than any other—and maybe all others combined!

The mystical quality I have described about music was readily apparent to me in the music of Gustav Mahler. In fact, in other instances of playing his music, even if it was not necessarily played well, it was still a mystical experience, because it was Mahler! If I felt this way about one particular composer—someone who knew that musical idolatry is not an option as a believer in Jesus Christ—surely others sensed this mystical, spiritual quality in the music of their revered composers. Other musicians, Christian and non-Christian, can find this devotion to music and musical composers a source of ultimate fulfillment, bordering on obsession. When the obsession focuses on the mystical experience of music rather than the connection to God through musical worship, music can become an idol. As Allen P. Ross points out, "The label 'idolatry' may be affixed to anything that fills our desires and devotions instead of God, anything that replaces God as the source of security and satisfaction in our lives, or anything that robs God of his proper place in our affections and commitments."[9]

When music becomes an idol in our lives, we attribute more worth to it than it deserves. Respected choral conductor and educator James Jordan demonstrates this inappropriate and disproportionate devotion to music in his book, *The Musician's Soul*: "To be a musician is a precious gift. Through our art, we can learn who we are, and where we live... We can also become blessed with the awareness that music grows out of the spirits that create it. If we listen profoundly to the music we make, it is the sound of that music that will lead us through our personal journey."[10]

This may sound innocuous at first glance. But where is our true identity found as Christians? Not in the music we make, but in the Lord we serve. Who leads us in life through our personal journey? It is the Spirit of God, not the spirits that create music. Jordan even uses the terminology of religion in a way that takes the glory due to God and gives it instead to music: "One's *innermost spiritual seat*, the place from which all musical impulse grows and is nourished, can only be accessed through time spent with one's self. Time for reflection. Time for listening to one's inner voice, which, when heard, speaks *ultimate truth* which is then reflected in music... I believe that within every artist is contained, deep within the 'soul,' *a fundamental set of truths*; without it, he or she would not be an artist."[11]

This vocabulary sounds appropriate in a spiritual discussion, but the target it modifies is misdirected. Jordan goes so far as to attribute to God a role in music, but his theology is most definitely skewed: "I have heard it said that 'God' is not a noun, but rather is a verb. The God for each of us that brings meaning to our life grows out of our own stillness. The 'God' that is a verb in all the music we make" (sic).[12]

This statement is an affront to the framework of orthodox Christianity. Worship is a verb, but God is most certainly a noun, a person. Our relationship to God, through our Lord and Savior, Jesus Christ, is what brings meaning to our life. Music is not an essential factor in this relationship, but it does provide an excellent vehicle to express our gratitude and worship to the "Source" of this meaning.

When music becomes more than a tool to express our devotion to God or a vehicle to give expression to our spiritual life, but instead becomes the focus of our devotion and the process of our spiritual pursuit, then we have crossed a line that moves music into the sphere of idolatry. Many serious musicians recognize that making music can be a spiritual experience. If there is a spiritual void in a musician's life because of no relationship to Jesus Christ as Savior and Lord, music can easily and understandably be appropriated to try to fill that void.

A glaring example of this is professional musician and bass player Victor L. Wooten, who actually subtitles his book, *The Music Lesson,* with "A Spiritual Search for Growth Through Music."[13] Wooten deifies music by always capitalizing the word and by maintaining that "Music is real, female, and you can have a relationship with her."[14] He describes a conversation he was having with Music, when she asked him to describe her. In a moment of spiritual ecstasy, feeling her energy all around him, he says "Love. Emotion. Beauty. Expression. Harmony. Communication. Spiritual. Natural. Vibrations. God!"[15] This is more than simple devotion to music. This is clearly unapologetic and blatant idolatry.

Even Augustine, the influential early church father (354–430), expressed his conflict with devotion to God and devotion to music in his *Confessions*:

> So often as I call to mind the tears I shed at the hearing of Thy Church songs, in the beginning of my recovered faith, yea, and at this very time, whenas I am moved not with the singing, but with the thing sung (when namely they are set off with a clear and suitable modulation), I then acknowledge the great use of this institution. Thus float I between peril and pleasure, and an approved profitable custom: inclined the more (though herein I pronounce no irrevocable opinion) to allow of the old usage of singing in the Church; that so by the delight taken in at the ears, the weaker minds be roused up into some feeling of devotion. And yet again, so oft as it befalls me to be moved

> with the voice rather than with the ditty, I confess myself to have grievously offended: at which time I wish rather not to have heard the music.[16]

Augustine recognized the danger inherent in the use of music in worship, when we are moved more "with the thing sung," rather than the God to whom we sing. It was such a peril for him that Augustine actually wished not to have even heard the music!

This inherent metaphysical appeal of music is illustrated by Jeremy S. Begbie, as he describes Arthur Schopenhauer's (1788–1860) philosophy of music: "Music peals forth the metaphysics of our own being, the crescendo, the climax, the crisis, the resolutions, of our own striving, impetuosity, peace, and the retardations and accelerations, the surging and passivity, the power and silence of things."[17] All these characteristics give music what Begbie describes as a "similar religious glow."[18] But at the same time, Begbie asks: "What kind of checks do we have against the idolatry of music? How can we distinguish adequately between encountering the divine and what is no more than an intensely emotional experience conveyed through music?"[19]

Musicians who succumb to this temptation to idolatry effectively obsess over music and their musical pursuits. Ezekiel 14:3 describes this human propensity for idolatry in this way: "Son of man, these men have set up their idols in their hearts and have put right before their faces the stumbling block of their iniquity." Music is continually before the face of most devoted musicians, but with it comes the potential to become a stumbling block. Referring to this verse, Keller explains that "God was saying that the human heart takes good things such as a successful career, love, material possessions, even family, and turns them into ultimate things. Our hearts deify them as the center of our lives, because, we think, they can give us significance and security, safety and fulfillment, if we attain them."[20]

All these things are respectable pursuits, including music, but none of them can be the source of our ultimate fulfillment. They will only disappoint if they are the sole source of our purpose in life. Only God can satisfy our greatest desire for fulfillment and purpose: "The Lord is my shepherd; I have everything I need" (Ps. 23:1, NLT).

One of the most comprehensive and profound definitions of idolatry is given by Harold Best in his book, *Unceasing Worship*: "Idolatry is the condition of self-deluded sovereignty by which we choose a god, assume it to be self-originating, craft a life system over which it is enthroned and then surrender to it, forgetting that its mastery is a figment of our imagination. In short, creature chooses creature and then deifies it."[21] Tim Keller defines an idol as "anything more important to you than God, anything that absorbs your heart and imagination more than God, anything you seek to give you what only God can give."[22] Can music really be an idol? Most definitely it can when it becomes the sole source of significance and fulfillment in a human life.

If God is the sovereign ruler of our life, he is effectively pushed off the throne as our hearts deify music, putting the creation in a role it does not inherently possess.

Anything that takes the place of God as our sole source of fulfillment and significance can be an idol, including music. The Bible is full of passages about idolatry. Music qualifies, not as the primary definition of an idol—"an image of a god, used as an object or instrument of worship"—but as the secondary definition: "any object of ardent or excessive devotion or admiration." Music is a good created thing, but when we turn it into the ultimate thing, putting creation in a role it does not inherently possess, we make it an idol. This "music of darkness" is a reflection of man's sinfulness and rebellion against God, resulting only in death.

In the next chapter I will explore the factors that contributed to this brazen musical idolatry. How did we transform music into an idol?

NOTES

[1]"You shall have no other gods before me" (Exod. 20:3, Deut. 5:7).

[2]Allen P. Ross, *Recalling the Hope of Glory: Biblical Worship from the Garden to the New Creation* (Grand Rapids: Kregel Publications, 2006), 311.

[3]Timothy Keller, *Counterfeit Gods: The Empty Promises of Money, Sex, and Power, and the Only Hope That Matters* (New York: Penguin Books, 2009), xiv.

[4]Ibid., 179.

[5]Harold M. Best, *Music Through the Eyes of Faith* (New York: HarperCollins Publishers, 1993), 49.

[6]Ibid., 48.

[7]Harold M. Best, *Unceasing Worship: Biblical Perspectives on Worship and the Arts* (Downers Grove, IL: InterVarsity Press, 2003), 163.

[8]Con Campbell, *Outreach and the Artist: Sharing the Gospel with the Arts* (Grand Rapids: Zondervan, 2013), 100.

[9]Ross, *Recalling the Hope of Glory,* 311.

[10]James Jordan, *The Musician's Soul* (Chicago: GIA Publications, Inc., 1999), 140-141.

[11]Ibid., 21-22 (emphasis mine).

[12]Ibid., 24.

[13]Victor L. Wooten, *The Music Lesson: A Spiritual Search for Growth Through Music* (New York: Berkley Books, 2006).

[14]Ibid., 2.

[15]Ibid., 253.

[16]R.W.S. Mendl, *The Divine Quest in Music* (London: Rockliff Publishing, 1957), 28.

[17]Jeremy S. Begbie, *Resounding Truth: Christian Wisdom in the World of Music* (Grand Rapids: Baker Academic, 2007), 151, quoting Israel Knox, *The Aesthetic Theories of Kant, Hegel, and Schopenhauer* (London: Thames & Hudson, 1958), 151.

[18]Ibid., 151.

[19]Ibid.

[20]Keller, *Counterfeit Gods,* xvi.

[21]Best, *Unceasing Worship,* 163.

[22]Keller, *Counterfeit Gods,* xix.

Chapter 4

The Transformation of Music into an Idol

How did we get from music, created for God's glory, to music actually receiving glory as an idol? I have spent most of my life making music—from piano lessons in elementary school; to band in middle school, high school, and college; to a career in music education and church music. It's not hard for me to see how easily music can become an idol in many musicians' lives. Making music can be a very fulfilling activity. It can give those involved a feeling of significance and security, especially if they are particularly good at it. In addition, there is an amazing camaraderie with other musicians when they make music together. It is remarkably similar to a religion, where the musical group is the congregation, the director is the pastor, the rehearsals are Bible studies, and the concerts are church services. The musicians are even encouraged to spend time practicing their individual musical part, with daily devotion! Thomas J. Terry and J. Ryan Lister offer this insight:

> Idols are relentless. They won't let go until they have all of who we are. The idol of creativity (i.e. music making) captures our attention with our own reflection and holds it there until all we can see is ourselves and our imaginative "genius." The world fades into the background, and our neighbors are there only to serve our personal interests. Sure, we want to entertain everyone, we want the audience to love us, and we want them to follow our every move. But it's often for no other reason than to earn their applause and ticket sales.[1]

In addition to the musical idolatry of the musician, there is also the passion of the masses for music—not necessarily those who make the music, but those who listen. Jeremy Begbie acknowledges that "a large part of the population spends considerable amounts of time (and money) seeking it out. A glance at the statistics of musical consumption in any Western country will confirm this."[2] Popular music artists have an intensely devoted following, with fan clubs, packed concerts, and audiences who know every word of their songs. Additionally, the masses are always looking for the next great musical superstar, as evidenced by the aptly titled, long-running TV show, *American Idol*.

We often loosely use the words "cult-like following" to describe this devotion of music fans to their favorite musicians. Sometimes this terminology becomes more reality than analogy. Consider the alternative rock band, Thirty Seconds to Mars, whose members have unapologetically embraced calling the devotion of their fans a cult. Their singer and guitarist, Jared Leto, has been called a prophet, as he dresses in all white, taking on a Jesus-like persona. This is disturbing, even to the secular media. A.C. Speed comments:

> Cult leaders start to feel very powerful as their followers hang onto their every word and praise the ground they walk on. Also, just look at the pictures of Jared Leto, he is very much taking on the role of an open armed Messiah. Dressed all in white with his biblical hair swooning his audience and being the centre of attention. Plus, everyone is dressed in white, it literally looks like a cult.[3]

As unbelievable as this may seem, it is a tragic reality in today's culture, as people seek to fill the God-shaped void in their life with blatant idolatry of music and musicians. This is not just a modern phenomenon. Begbie cites the idolatrous views of music by German Romantic author and composer E.T.A. Hoffman (1776–1822): "instrumental music, stripped of external trappings such as words, becomes a means of 'striving for inner spirituality,' for the divine life that resides within."[4] I have already addressed the spiritual nature of music, and that mystical allure, combined with the natural God-shaped void in each individual, which makes music a huge temptation to idolatry. Many unchurched musicians substitute music for God, but for those who attend church, often devotion to music draws them to weekly worship, rather than devotion to God.

My daughter-in-law, a recent graduate vocal performance student, is often hired by local churches as a professional singer. A devoted Christian, many times she returns from these experiences disillusioned with the mindset of the music leaders in these churches. They speak highly of their devotion to their musical pursuits, but there is little or no evidence of devotion to Christ. Their motivation for ministry is strictly musical—in many cases, with no apparent evidence of motivation to exalt Christ through their music. Their lifestyles outside of worship bear witness to this, as they are often indistinguishable from those who are unchurched and not devoted to Christ. This is a real symptom of musical idolatry, and alarmingly, in churches that actually appear to be Christian houses of worship.

Immediate accessibility of music also contributes to this problem of musical idolatry. "The revolution in digital technology and Internet communication availability has played a critical role here," according to Begbie, "opening up an unprecedented flood of constant access to music."[5] We live in a culture where music is always one click away—in our homes, in our cars, and on our cell phones. We watch movies and TV shows about the lives of our favorite musicians, and are intensely interested in every little detail about them. We spend our money on their recordings and even more money to attend their concerts. There are even other musicians who try to emulate their favorite musicians, in the form of cover bands or impersonators, and we spend our money to hear them!

The recording industry has greatly affected the accessibility of music to the masses and of musical careers to the masses. Because of the technology available in recording studios, almost anyone with minor musical talent can make a respectable recorded album. Many of these artists never sing live, as it would expose their musical faults. If they do attempt to sing live, we witness their inadequacies or else see them simply lip-syncing with their recording made with technology that makes them sound better than they actually are. Musical artists and groups who actually sound good in a live concert setting seem to be the exception in today's technology-driven musical environment.

Another characteristic of music is its pervasiveness throughout out modern world. We simply cannot get away from it. Omnipresent is a term used to describe a divine attribute of God: "present in all places at the same time."[6] Begbie quotes F.A. Biocca, saying "Most noticeable to many was the *sudden omnipresence of music*."[7] Begbie points out that "through sound technology, music has come to *surround* us, some would say invade us, as never before."[8] "To use what is now a cliché, music has become a soundtrack for life. We no longer need to search it out—music will search us out through walls, ceiling speakers, on United Airlines as *Rhapsody in Blue,* through that teenager's earphones on the other side of the bus."[9] Through its ever-present nature in our culture, music has taken on a ubiquitous character, resembling the omnipresence of almighty God.

We might be inclined to assume that this idolatry is exclusively a problem outside the church, and dismiss the possibility that it could actually occur inside the church. Unfortunately, the church is frequently guilty of emulating the culture around it, and music is no exception. Marva J. Dawn expresses "the anguish of looking for a congregation and discovering, to my distress, how extensively society's idolatries have invaded the Church and its worship."[10] Just as music can become an idol outside the church for both musicians and those who listen to music, those inside the church can be guilty of the same misplaced devotion, although seemingly unaware of this deceptive idolatry.

I have mentioned the possibility that churches may sometimes hire a music director simply for that person's musical qualifications, with no apparent interest in their spiritual walk, theological understanding, and training. My daughter-in-law has observed this phenomenon in churches where she has served as a paid singer.

They often hire a musically qualified individual, such as a professor at a local college or university, with no regard or apparent interest in the candidate's spiritual state. This can be true in the recruitment of the entire worship team in some churches, as they try to assemble the highest level of musicianship possible, totally ignoring the spiritual state of some of the individuals. Remembering that the Old Testament worship leaders in the Tabernacle and the Temple were from the tribe of Levi, we see these Levites set apart for the worship of God by Moses:

> The Lord said to Moses: "Take the Levites from among all the Israelites and make them ceremonially clean. To purify them, do this: Sprinkle the water of cleansing on them; then have them shave their whole bodies and wash their clothes. And so they will purify themselves. Have them take a young bull with its grain offering of the finest flour mixed with olive oil; then you are to take a second young bull for a sin offering. Bring the Levites to the front of the tent of meeting and assemble the whole Israelite community. You are to bring the Levites before the Lord, and the Israelites are to lay their hands on them. Aaron is to present the Levites before the Lord as a wave offering from the Israelites, so that they may be ready to do the work of the Lord." (Num. 8:5-11, NIV)

This passage of Scripture expresses the commitment to purity and consecration in the lives of the Levites. In many ways, worship leaders in today's churches—both paid and volunteer—are modern-day Levites. They should therefore be set apart for service, living pure and holy lives. Our preoccupation with their musical qualifications, rather than their spiritual state, is disturbing. Because of this relative lack of spiritual maturity on the part of many worship leaders, they naturally spend much more time preparing for each Sunday musically than preparing spiritually, through prayer and Bible study. Block maintains that "churches must hold ministers responsible for music to the same moral and spiritual standards as they do for those who proclaim the Word... Like the priests of Israel, everything about their daily conduct, as well as their demeanor and appearance before God's people, should inspire respect for the ministry and especially reverence for God."[11]

For those serving in the music ministry of churches, they often see their devotion to Christ solely as their musical service to the church, to the exclusion of personal prayer and Bible study, participation in a small group Bible study, or serving in any other type of ministry. These individuals can come to church, perform their musical service, and leave, feeling they have done their spiritual duty while ignoring many other crucial forms of devotion to God. In this situation, music can be the driving force in their Christian experience, and whether they realize it or not, I submit that it has potentially become the sole recipient of their spiritual devotion.

Just like those outside the church who are not musicians but listen to music, those inside the church can also be guilty of misplaced devotion when it comes to music. Many of our contemporary worship leaders and artists have cult-like followings, equal to any popular secular artist. Those persons devoted to their music collect their recordings and attend as many of their concerts/worship gatherings as possible. These Christian musicians assume celebrity status from those who listen to and follow their music. Marva Dawn remarks, "Sometimes congregations who feature lead musicians and singers are tempted to put them on pedestals, with the result that worshipers simply let them perform and no longer participate in communal singing."[12] Congregational participation in worship suffers because of this form of idolatry. Respected worship leader Stephen Miller, in his appropriately titled book *Worship Leaders: We Are Not Rock Stars*, describes this phenomenon as symptomatic of our culture:

> The problem is that for many, the tools of worship have become a substitute for actual worship of Christ. It's not necessarily their fault. It's a result of the emotionally driven celebrity culture we have created and modeled for them in church. When a leader is talented and charismatic in personality, we tend to put them on a proverbial pedestal and blur the line between admiration and worship, between imitating them as they imitate Christ and substituting them for Christ. With music, this is all the more dangerous because we are dealing with a naturally emotional medium.[13]

This emotional medium of music can often be mistaken as worship. A.W. Tozer offers this observation: "Some mistake the music of religion as true worship because music elevates the mind. Music raises the heart to near rapture. Music can lift our feelings into ecstasy. Music has a purifying, purging effect upon us. So it's possible to fall into a happy and elevated state of mind with a vague notion about God and imagine we're worshiping God when we're doing nothing of the sort."[14]

In addition to mistaking the emotion of music with worship, there is also the danger of confusing the act of worship with the object of our worship. D.A. Carson speculates, "One sometimes wonders if we are beginning to worship *worship* rather than worship *God*... it's a bit like those who begin by admiring the sunset and soon begin to admire themselves admiring the sunset."[15] Harold Best maintains that "idolatry is the chief enemy of the most fervently worshiping Christians, even to the extent that some of us may end up worshiping worship."[16] As ludicrous as that sounds, it is a real possibility in modern churches. People are sometimes drawn to churches because of their outstanding worship music, instead of being drawn to the exalted Savior they worship. There is a fine line of distinction between the worshipers' devotion to Christ and their devotion to the church and the church's worship and music.

In many worship settings Christians not only exalt the music, but they also exalt themselves as they seek to worship through music. If you examine the lyrics of many of our contemporary worship songs, this increased emphasis on "me-oriented" worship is disturbing. Consider this insightful observation by Robert E. Webber: "Me-oriented worship is the result of a culturally driven worship. When worship is situated in the culture and not in the story of God, worship becomes focused on the self. It becomes narcissistic ... much of our worship has shifted from a focus on God and God's story to a focus on me and my story."[17]

We need to remember that Jesus' death on the cross accomplished everything required by God for our justification. As John Risbridger puts it, "We have no need to impress God with extravagant claims about the extent of our heart's devotion."[18] Risbridger elaborates: "I wonder if I sometimes detect this perceived need in 'worship songs' which make very extravagant claims of devotion to God, while articulating little if anything about the goodness of God which might provoke such devotion."[19] This perceived need to express our devotion to God in our worship songs can be misapplied as trying to earn God's acceptance, focusing on our works, and adding to what Christ has already accomplished for us through his death on the cross. While we are focused on the greatness of our devotion, we miss the greatness of God!

This me-oriented worship is most clearly reflected in songs that seem to express a romantic relationship with Christ, songs that are prevalent in today's evangelistic culture. Robert A. Myers points out that "modern ideas of romance are, by their very nature, self-focused. We 'fall in love' to find happiness and our true selves."[20] The solution to this fixation on self is to include more songs with corporate pronouns (we, us, ours). Songs that express individual worship are not necessarily wrong; they are just too prevalent. We need a healthy balance with songs that also communicate our corporate identity with other believers.

In addition to the narcissistic bent to much of our modern worship, there is also an unhealthy focus on the methodology of worship, rather than a focus on the holy object of our worship. This focus on methodology most often involves an emphasis on style in worship, specifically the style of the music. Such an emphasis on an aspect of worship that is constantly changing (style), rather than on worship that brings us into the presence of a holy God, exposes music and musical style as an object of idolatry. Frank S. Page and L. Lavon Gray offer this insight and the examples that follow: "Many spend much more time promoting a style of worship than encouraging people to stand in the presence of God. And a lot of us have bought into the idea!

This coming weekend countless people will leave our worship services and comment, 'I loved the worship today,' when they really mean they loved the music."[21]

This emphasis on worship method effectively makes music an idol, and is all too common in our churches today. Consider the following examples offered by Page and Gray of how many churches promote their worship services, focusing primarily on music style and the musicians or musical forces leading the worship:[22]

> At 11:00 a.m. each Sunday, you can come experience contemporary worship.
>
> Our contemporary worship service provides an opportunity to experience energetic, band-oriented, spiritually fulfilling praise and worship in a modern environment.
>
> Sunday at 9:00 a.m. is our traditional worship service. This service is characterized by the hymns we've come to appreciate as a part of our heritage and faith, as well as by classic choruses, and will be accompanied by our dynamic celebration choir and orchestra.
>
> Experience our contemporary service. This service is led by a progressive worship band, and uses material from a variety of worship sources, including songs written by our own team of worship leaders.
>
> Each Sunday morning service incorporates different musical styles: 8:30 a.m. traditional with hymns and songs of the faith led by choir and orchestra, organ, and piano; 9:45 a.m. contemporary with energizing and uplifting music led by band, choir, and vocalists; and 11:15 a.m. modern with passionate, upbeat, band-led, creative media-rich experience.

Notice that in each of these examples the emphasis is on the methodology of worship, specifically the music or musical forces. The words or descriptions focus on style: contemporary, band-driven, modern, traditional, hymns, classic choruses, choir and orchestra, progressive worship band, organ and piano, etc. None of these are bad things in themselves, but nothing is said about experiencing God. The focus is on the *method* of worship, not the *object* of worship.

Harold Best identifies three idols, related to music, that have plagued the church throughout the centuries: the idols of quality, effectiveness, and stasis (or stability).[23] Quality (or beauty) becomes an idol when we make a judgment call on what is and is not appropriate for worship, based on our perception of what is beautiful or "quality music." This particular idol is most related to the issue of style in our worship music, and is totally dependent on subjective opinion. I have heard the testimony of professional singers, hired to sing in churches, who tell me that the church music leaders often take more pride in the excellence of their music or the excellence of their musicians than the greatness of the Savior they worship. They challenge their hired musicians to give their best for the sake of the quality of their music or the reputation of the church, rather than motivating them to offer their best for their Savior. Whenever we judge the beauty of music to be more important than the focus of our music in worship, we are guilty of idolatry.

Beauty is therefore subservient to God and to Jesus Christ, who is "the way, and the truth, and the life" (John 14:6). This relationship between beauty and truth is articulated well by author N.T. Wright: "What we must also rule out … is the idea that beauty gives us direct access to God, to 'the divine,' or to a transcendent realm of any sort. The fact that the music is clearly designed to go with the larger whole gives us no direct clue as to what the larger whole might be… The beauty of the natural world is, at best, the echo of a voice, not the voice itself."[24]

The elevation of quality in worship and the snobbery associated with it can extend in both directions. There is actually an elitism that can be experienced in contemporary worship that resembles the elitism in more traditional worship expressions. The leaders of these modern worship services can actually take pride in the skill of their musicians without any classical music training. This pride in natural ability and the ability to "play by ear" can exalt music and musicians in worship just as much as those who pride themselves on higher art forms and musical training. It is not a bad thing to emphasize musical excellence in worship, but when it is emphasized over experiencing God's presence in worship, we can be guilty of the sin of idolatry.

Best's second idol is effectiveness. The idol of effectiveness bases the value of music only on the results it produces, such as the audience it draws in worship or the decisions it influences. Best observes, "Here is where artistic action and thinned-out versions of evangelization and seeker sensitivity can be comfortable bedfellows."[25] Such a results-oriented attitude toward the value of music gives music more credit than it deserves. Marva Dawn calls this "the Idolatry of Numbers and Success."[26] She points out that with this idolatry, "The danger to the Church is enormous and, strangely, often not obvious. Quality suffers when the main concern is quantity."[27] We must remember that Jesus did not measure success by how many disciples he had, and he warned his disciples that "the way is narrow" (Matt. 7:14). This idol also ignores the role of the Holy Spirit in our worship. The Bible is clear that without the Holy Spirit (John 3:5), no one comes to saving faith and is able to worship in

Spirit and in truth (John 4:23-24). To judge our worship based on effectiveness alone totally excludes the influence of the Holy Spirit.

The third idol operates on the premise that if music has worked well in the past, we should not change it. This is the idol of stasis or stability. Most every church deals with a certain contingent of the congregation who is resistant to change. These members have a certain preference for a style of music that inevitably leads to a fear of variety. But the Psalms encourage us to "sing to Him a new song" (Ps. 33:3), rather than saying "Not in my style, therefore I cannot worship."[28] Dawn identifies this idolatry as "the Way We've Never Done It Before."[29] This idolatry of traditionalism can be summed up in the stereotypical seven last words of the church: "We never did it that way before." We must avoid allowing worship to become boring and stale, and instead heed the words of Christ in Mark 2:22 and Luke 5:37 to "put new wine into fresh wineskins." Old forms can be devoid of life, but the Spirit of God can breathe new life into our worship, if we are open to change.

Many churches have great ostensible reputations for their outstanding worship services, drawing large crowds, but in many cases worship typically means music and only music. As important as music is in biblical worship, music is not the same as worship. It is only one of many elements of worship. The other more traditional and historical parts of worship (preaching, prayer, communion) are often not considered as essential elements when many churches formulate their worship services. Worshipers in these situations lose sight of the centrality of the Word and Table, which in the early church constituted the established structure of worship (along with prayer and fellowship): "They were continually devoting themselves to the apostles' teaching and to fellowship, to the breaking of bread and to prayer" (Acts 2:42).

Noted author and expert on worship, Robert E. Webber, maintains that from this earliest of Scripture references about the pattern of worship in the early church, a consistent fourfold pattern emerged in the early church model:

1. Gathering—the assembling of the people for worship
2. Word—Scripture readings and the preaching of God's Word
3. Table—breaking bread and pouring wine, with thanksgiving, as a response to God's Word
4. Sending—the people depart to love and serve the Lord[30]

These elements of early Christian worship must remain central in contemporary worship, with God's Word as the unchanging focal point, the Lord's Supper as the most appropriate response to God's Word, and the whole service bathed in prayer and overflowing with Christian fellowship. Music can be an effective tool in worship that can declare God's Word, enhance the observance of the Lord's Supper, voice the congregation's prayer, and unite the fellowship of the body in praise of almighty God. When music stands alone in worship, it is in danger of becoming an idol in the church. The priority of Word and Table must be emphasized to correct this deficiency. The full dynamic of biblical worship is the most effectual corrective for unbalanced worship that emphasizes music disproportionately.

Our music-oriented culture, with its idolization of music and musicians, has contributed greatly to the idolatry of music. Examples of this include the pop music phenomena, personified in the TV show *American Idol,* and groups such as Thirty Seconds to Mars, with their literal cult-like following. Sadly, this type of idolatry can manifest itself inside the church, especially as the church emulates contemporary culture. Narcissism and an unhealthy emphasis on methodology in worship add to this idolatry. Music should never be the sole expression of our corporate worship. Instead, we must strive to restore the historic fourfold pattern of worship: Gathering, Word, Table, and Sending.

Idolatry of music is a real problem, due to a variety of influences. In the next chapter I will share the testimonies of two individuals who have witnessed musical idolatry, from two different perspectives.

NOTES

[1]Thomas J. Terry and J. Ryan Lister, *Images and Idols: Creativity for the Christian Life* (Chicago: Moody Publishers, 2018), 86.

[2]Jeremy S. Begbie, *Resounding Truth: Christian Wisdom in the World of Music* (Grand Rapids: Baker Academic, 2007), 16.

[3]A.C. Speed, "Jared Leto has started a CULT on an island and his followers call him 'Prophet,'" Raw Music TV: Music, News, Gaming and Culture, September 18, 2019, https://www.rawmusictv.com/article/amp/2019/Jared-Leto-has-started-a-CULT-on-an-island-and-his-followers-call-him-Prophet (accessed September 23, 2019).

[4]Begbie, *Resounding Truth,* 151.

[5]Ibid., 16.

[6]Webster's New World College Dictionary, 4th ed., s.v. "omnipresent."

[7]Begbie, *Resounding Truth,* 34, quoting F.A. Bioca, "The Pursuit of Sound: Radio, Perception, and Utopia in the Early 20th Century," *Media, Culture, and Society* 10 (1988): 61-62.

[8]Ibid., 33.

[9]Ibid., 34.

[10]Marva Dawn, *Reaching Out without Dumbing Down: A Theology of Worship for the Turn-of-the-Century Culture* (Grand Rapids: Eerdmans Publishing Co., 1995), 42.

[11]Daniel I. Block, *For the Glory of God: Recovering a Biblical Theology of Worship* (Grand Rapids: Baker Academic, 2014), 245.

[12]Dawn, *Reaching Out Without Dumbing Down,* 51.

[13]Stephen Miller, *Worship Leaders: We Are Not Rock Stars* (Chicago: Moody Publishers, 2013), 16.

[14]A.W. Tozer, *Worship: The Reason We Were Created—Collected Insights from A.W. Tozer* (Chicago: Moody Publishers, 2017), 58-59.

[15]D.A. Carson, *Worship by the Book,* (Grand Rapids: Zondervan, 2002), 31.

[16]Harold M. Best, *Unceasing Worship: Biblical Perspectives on Worship and the Arts* (Downers Grove, IL: InterVarsity Press, 2003), 163.

[17]Robert E. Webber, *The Divine Embrace: Recovering the Passionate Spiritual Life* (Grand Rapids: Baker Books, 2006), 231.

[18]John Risbridger, *The Message of Worship: Celebrating the Glory of God in the Whole Life, The Bible Speaks Today,* ed. Derek Tidball (Downers Grove, IL: InterVarsity Press, 2015), 129.

[19]Ibid.

[20]Robert A. Myers, *Strategic Portraits: People and Movements That Shaped Evangelical Worship* (Jacksonville, FL: Webber Institute Books, 2019), 75-76.

[21]Frank S. Page and L. Lavon Gray, *Hungry for Worship: Challenges and Solutions for Today's Church* (Birmingham, AL: New Hope Publishers, 2014), Kindle version, location 231.

[22]Examples from Page and Gray, *Hungry for Worship,* location 337.

[23]Best, *Unceasing Worship,* 169.

[24]N.T. Wright, *Simply Christian: Why Christianity Makes Sense* (New York: HarperOne, 2006), 43.

[25]Ibid., 168.

[26]Dawn, *Reaching Out without Dumbing Down,* 51.

[27]Ibid.

[28]Best, *Unceasing Worship,* 169.

[29]Dawn, *Reaching Out without Dumbing Down,* 47.

[30]Robert E. Webber, *Worship Old and New* (Grand Rapids: Zondervan, 1994), 150.

Chapter 5

Two Testimonies of Musical Idolatry

I now offer two individual testimonies, one from a young jazz musician who was convicted that he was guilty of musical idolatry and the other from a classically trained college voice professor who routinely observes this idolatry in her students and colleagues.

As a church instrumental music director, one of the groups I direct at my church is a youth orchestra that is open to all high school instrumentalists. Many families with multiple children have participated in this program through the years, including the Fulkerson family. All four of the Fulkerson children are very talented string players, but their third child, Will, is an exceptional musician. When Will became involved with the youth orchestra, he was a decent violinist, but when his mother asked me to consider using him on piano, I realized that his true giftedness was piano playing.

Will is now a young adult, having graduated with a jazz studies degree from Florida State University. Because of his health challenges, his testimony is a difficult one to hear, but it is a perfect example of how music can become an idol, even in the life of a believer in Jesus Christ. Here is his testimony, used with his permission:

> I'm going to be sharing my testimony in regard to music becoming an idol, just being a musician and my current identity in Christ, with all its goodness.
>
> I started playing music very early on. I was four when I started piano lessons, seven when I was doing violin and kind of started playing other string instruments in my early teens—always with an emphasis on piano. I had that natural thing, that natural gift, as some people would say, where I just had a natural inclination for music. I remember just picking out songs by ear as a kid, alongside with my classical lessons. And I loved playing stuff by ear. I eventually got into jazz when I was in eighth grade. Even as a kid, I was used to being gifted in music. I was used to people knowing that and for having the spotlight on me in those ways, even at talent shows in middle school and in a band in high school. I had my identity, even early on, in being that good piano player, that good musician. And I liked the attention, of course. Who wouldn't?
>
> I kind of grew up being the best musician in the room. I got into jazz and went to college at Florida State University. That whole attitude continued in college. My second year I beat out a grad student to be in the top jazz

combo. There I was, only 20 years old, and this grad student was 29, and they placed me above him. I even got to perform in New York City. I was also the first call for most of the jazz gigs. All of the professors would call me first if they needed a piano player.

All of this contributed to a growing ego. And in addition to that, my first year and my second year in college, I wasn't very kind to people who weren't that good at jazz. This actually is way more common than you'd think. Many people in the jazz world equate musical ability with overall value. And even if they wouldn't admit it, they act in a superior way that kind of looks down on others. I regret that now and it's just crazy, but that's what was going on in college.

By this time in my story, I'm like 21 or 22, and at that point I was just totally using my musical ability and the respect of other musicians to fuel my short-term happiness and pride. But it's just never enough. And deep down, I was beginning to realize that no amount of status, skill, or respect can make you feel good enough about yourself that you're ultimately satisfied.

Despite all of this, I was saved. I got saved when I was 18 on a mission trip to Peru with my home church, Johnson Ferry Baptist Church in Marietta, Georgia. But despite establishing this identity, I guess you could say I walked away from the Lord and totally idolized music and my ego and my pride for a number of years in college before I finally came back to him.

No matter how good people think you are in music, you must realize that it doesn't ever satisfy. The joy of making music is a gift from God. But doing it with pride, it's never enough. You're never going to be the best in the world. It's just never enough. You just always want more and more and more, and it just doesn't satisfy. I finally started to realize this through the Lord just tugging at my heart, which gets to the heart of my story.

Thankfully—looking back, I can say thankfully—the Lord allowed a condition called focal dystonia in my hands and some other related physical problems. Basically, it's a movement disorder I have now: my fingers started twitching and my forearms got super, super tight, to the point where I had to stop playing gigs. The one part of my life I thought that I was in control of and responsible for—that being music—the Lord just showed me that no, I wasn't in control and that he's in control and that he gives and he takes away.

The Lord just took away that physical ability to play. So, I'm effectively out of commission when it comes to playing gigs. So, the Lord took away that which I was idolizing. It was my identity. I realized that my identity was in music. And when the Lord took away my ability to play, I basically was left identity-less. I couldn't continue to feed my pride and my self-worth with the admiration of others and their affirmation that I was this great jazz pianist.

So, I needed to consider an identity switch. I was saved, but I wasn't walking with the Lord. I knew deep down that Jesus was the only thing that could satisfy. I knew it. I had knowledge. I just had never really full-fledged, 100 percent surrendered. I understood the concept, but I had never experienced it. So, I just gave the Lord everything, in the middle of my brokenness, in the middle of what seemed like a terrible tragedy to me. I had nothing to cling to except for the Lord.

I just latched onto the Lord, saying, "You know what, if I'm going to be a Christian, I'm going to actually do this." Because I knew you have to either be 100 percent for the Lord or it doesn't work. You can't just have one foot in and one foot out. So, the Lord just broke me, using my hand injury, to the point where I surrendered everything, and the Lord has been teaching me humility ever since.

I still have to work on that every day, specifically my pride. Christ is concerned with our hearts. And that's illustrated by the fact that the Lord did not hesitate to take away my ability to play, knowing that it would bring me closer to him. I mean, that's obviously way more important.

So, what I found out that was really satisfying was realizing I was nothing apart from Christ. Seeing the depth of his grace and love for me, that is what was satisfying. Knowing that he is in control of my life, that's what's satisfying, way more satisfying—way more than trying to impress people with my music.

In the Apostle Paul's letters he says to die to yourself or die to the flesh. I need to stop being an advocate for myself—where it's all about me, me, me, me, me. There's a lot more joy in advocating for Christ compared to advocating for myself. And it takes a lot of pressure off of me, too. Because it's just tiring always trying to advocate for yourself. It should be about Christ.

Christ is everything, and all that I have comes from him. I trust him with my life, and I know I'm in good hands. So, it's the best. I'm daily reminded of the forgiveness I need, and it keeps me humble. What really helps with staying humble is just reading Scripture and spending time with the Lord and realizing how broken and sinful I am and every day that I need God's grace.

To shatter my view of myself, I start with comparing myself to Christ and I come up short. The closer you get to the light, the more you see your own darkness. I'm daily reminded of the forgiveness I need and just the grace, restoration, and renewal that the Lord has showed in my life. Now

> I'm actually thankful that I got focal dystonia, simply because it broke me free from the never-ending cycle of self-fulfillment and it brought me closer to Christ.
>
> My prayer is that the Lord would do whatever he needs to do in your life to get you to surrender to the Lord, because that's where you're ultimately going to find satisfaction. That's where you're going to be your true self, where you're going to be who the Lord has called you to be. If anything is in the way, if anything is sitting on the throne of your heart, I pray that the Lord will do whatever it takes, by any means necessary, to reorder your heart. I'm thankful he did for me.
>
> That's my testimony. I still have to just wake up daily, die to myself, put myself in my place, and know that I'm a sinner. But I've been forgiven and the Lord loves me and Jesus died on the cross for my sins, so that I need to have humility and I need to forgive others. I just desperately need the Lord, because he's the only thing that can ultimately satisfy. I have to surrender every day. It's not a one-and-done exercise. You have to surrender every day. Even though there's a lot of pain in my story, the Lord is good and I trust him. I trust him in every way.

This testimony of Will Fulkerson, who was guilty of idolizing music through his pursuit of jazz studies in college, is real-life evidence of the serious temptation of musicians toward musical idolatry. It also demonstrates the proper response of conviction of sin, repentance, and renewed devotion to Christ.

Jana Young is an associate professor of music at Kennesaw State University, the second largest university in the State of Georgia. She is an accomplished vocal professor and a committed Christian, impacting her students both musically and personally. She speaks into the subjects of narcissism and the idolatry of self, along with the idolatry of composers and quality, all addressed in the previous chapter:

> In teaching young aspiring singers, I often come across those students who feel they have no worth unless they are chosen for the solos, lead roles, and resulting accolades of their peers. Most measure how worthy they are by the amount of applause they receive at the end of each performance. Many students and young artists would claim to be self-made performers: "I put in the time, I worked and improved, I owe the success to me, my hard work, and to my decisions." I have to remind everyone studying with me that they are the third leg of a stool, lending an expressive voice to represent the particular poet and composer. All three of these—poet/lyricist, composer,

> and artist—work in concert simply because God allows this and because he has gifted us in this way with ability and talent. To quote Rick Warren, "it's not about you."[1] We must use those gifts to give worship in return.
>
> I am a voice teacher and professional singer, and I remind students, as well as myself, that God has given us the breath to worship him. This singing profession is about worship, even if it isn't a sacred song. The act of worshiping while one sings takes the focus off the composer, lyricist, and the singer. This realization is incredibly freeing.
>
> Perfection cannot be reached by human means, but many singers strive to perfection. They want nothing less. I often ask them, "Who will be the judge if a performance is perfect or not?" Our imperfect performance is made perfect through him who died for us.
>
> One important point to keep in mind is that a career is a lifetime of performing, with a long, slow crescendo and an arching phrase. We, as performers, need to see our body of work and the positive direction of its trajectory pointing to the God who gave us life and a song to sing.
>
> Giving God our best, while we practice, while we perform, and while we teach, will result in the sweetest sound and the most significant performances of our lives. Being thankful for the songs and the ability to be expressive is a wonderful gift. When we singers realize who we are worshiping and why we are worshiping, our artistic lives will take off and our songs will become pleasing to the Lord. What a wonderful opportunity to worship!

I truly appreciate both Will Fulkerson and Jana Young for lending their unique testimonies to this book on musical idolatry. Will risked being vulnerable, by sharing his profound, personal story of God's work in his life. Not only is he an example of someone who was guilty of making music an idol, but he is also an example of someone who was convicted of that sin and then repented and restored music to its proper perspective, with Christ back as the focus of his life.

Jana showed us through her mentoring and teaching experience some of the characteristic idolatries she encounters in her profession as a college voice teacher. These idolatries include narcissism (idolatry of self) and the idolatry of composers, in addition to the idolatry of quality. At the same time, she demonstrates her own God-honoring perspective, as a follower of Christ in a secular setting. It is possible, although difficult, to be pleasing to the Lord while serving him in the secular music world.

In the next chapter we will look at an interesting concept related to idolatry: becoming what we worship.

NOTE

[1]Rick Warren, *The Purpose Driven Life: What on Earth Am I Here For?* (Grand Rapids: Zondervan, 2012), 21.

Chapter 6

Becoming What We Worship—Even Music

When considering the effects of idolatry on a human life, we need to consider two very thought-provoking, almost identical verses in the Book of Psalms: "Those who make them will become like them, (yes,) everyone who trusts in them" (115:8, 135:18).

In both Psalm 115 and 135, the psalmist has been describing the idols of the nations, specifically that they are blind, deaf, and dumb. Then the psalmist makes the astute observation that "those who make them will become like them." In G.K. Beale's book, *We Become What We Worship*, he explains this concept: "These worshipers become as spiritually void and lifeless as the idols they committed themselves to."[1] Beale identifies this as "sensory-organ malfunction,"[2] resulting not in physical but spiritual insensitivity, "as spiritually insensitive and lifeless as the idols."[3] Charles H. Spurgeon quotes Robert Bellarmine, essentially affirming the same concept in his commentary on the Psalms: "they neither see nor hear the things that pertain to salvation, the things that only are worth seeing."[4]

Another related Scripture passage on this subject is Isaiah 6. After a profound encounter with a holy God, Isaiah is convicted of his sin, offered forgiveness by God, then accepts God's invitation to go and speak for God to sinful Israel (vv. 1-8). But instead of offering the same forgiveness he has received, he is instructed to speak of God's judgment:

> Go and tell this people:
> "Keep on listening, but do not perceive;
> Keep on looking, but do not understand."
> Render the hearts of this people insensitive,
> Their ears dull,
> And their eyes dim,
> Otherwise they might see with their eyes,
> Hear with their ears,
> Understand with their hearts,
> And return and be healed. (vv. 9-10)

Apparent in this passage is Israel's sin of idol worship. As a result of their idolatry, the Israelites became like their idols, with all their limitations. They were deaf, blind, and stupid. Isaiah's role then was one of announcing God's judgment, in hopes that Israel would repent and return to worship of the one true God.

How should we relate these insights from Scripture to music as an idol? First, we need to realize that music is an inanimate object by itself—devoid of sight, hearing, and speech without human influence. God is ultimately the creator of music, but humans also assist in that creation by composing and arranging musical compositions. Therefore, according to C.J.H. Wright, making music an idol "blurs the distinction between the Creator God and the creation. This both damages creation (including ourselves) and diminishes the glory of the Creator."[5]

We also need to consider the attitudes and terminology used by musicians who idolize music. Music idolaters often say "it's all about the music," while Christians say "it's all about Jesus." Another phrase that I've often heard from devoted musicians is the admonition to "be the music." This is remarkably similar to the scriptural concept in Psalms: those who trust in an idol will become like them! Lest you think this is not too common, consider these words from Victor L. Wooten, as he visualizes Music (with a capital M and female) speaking to him: "Remember," she said, "play me all you want, but you must know this: it is only when you allow *me* to play *you* that you will know me completely because then we will be one and the same."[6]

Being "one and the same" with music is another way of saying we become like the music. It is union with an inanimate object, a created thing that was never designed for that relationship with humankind. Choral conductor James Jordan also reflects this dynamic in his vocabulary: "The task of an artist, whether you be a conductor, a recital singer, or a choir member at church, is to understand that *your music is what you are, or who you know yourself to be.*"[7] This perspective on being or becoming the music is reflected in both popular music (with Victor Wooten) and traditional or classical music (with James Jordan), with equally alarming consequences. In the conclusion to his book, Beale puts this all in proper perspective:

> The principle is this: *What we revere, we resemble, either for ruin or restoration.* To commit ourselves to some part of the creation more than the Creator is idolatry. And when we worship something in creation, we become like it, as spiritually lifeless and insensitive to God as a piece of wood, rock or stone. We become spiritually blind, deaf and dumb even though we have physical eyes and ears. If we commit ourselves to something that does not have God's Spirit, to that degree we will be lacking the Spirit. We will be like ancient Israel.[8]

Israel's idolatry focused primarily on false gods and images or representations of those gods. Our idols today may be more sophisticated, but no less grievous. They still are lifeless substitutes for the living God of the universe.

Richard Lints presents a unique perspective in his book, *Identity and Idolatry: The Image of God and Its Inversion,*[9] based on these verses in Genesis 1:

> Then God said, "Let us make man in Our image, according to Our likeness; and let him rule over the fish of the sea and over the birds of the sky and over the cattle and over all the earth, and over every creeping thing that creeps on the earth." God created man in His own image, in the image of God He created him; male and female He created them. (vv. 26-27)

Lints begins with this biblical concept of *imago Dei* (Latin for "image of God") and describes "the unique relationship between humans and God."[10] He points out that idolatry effectively turns *imago Dei* upside down when humans "replace their Creator with something in the created order."[11] "Idolatry was the conceptual 'turning upside down' of the originally intended relationship of image to original."[12] John Risbridger explains: "The Bible is adamant that the living God cannot be faithfully represented by a lifeless statue, but that he has created human beings—into whom he breathed the 'breath of life' (Gen. 2:7)—in his own likeness, to be his image within creation, the representatives of his rule."[13] This is *imago Dei.*

Once *imago Dei* is turned upside down, the remedy for this idolatry is to "invert the inversion,"[14] as Lints says, and focus on the perfect image of God found in Christ Jesus. "In Christ the Creator has entered creation and thereby recreated the cosmic order after his image."[15] This concept of Christ as the perfect image of God is supported by multiple passages in the New Testament, but specifically these two Scriptures: "...Christ, who is the image of God" (2 Cor. 4:4) and "He is the image of the invisible God, the firstborn of all creation" (Col. 1:15).

This focus on Christ, the perfect image of God, assists in turning the story upside down. The remedy then for our idolatry is to "fix our eyes on Jesus, the author and perfecter of our faith" (Heb. 12:2). Risbridger confirms: "Jesus is the perfect human being who bears the flawless image of God" and "he *is* (eternally) the image of God after which we were ourselves fashioned."[16] Speaking in musical terms, Reggie M. Kidd suggests that Jesus redeems sinners by saving "people who before knowing him have sung only dirty or idolatrous ditties. Jesus purges the idolatrous aspects of a culture's music and focuses the yearning for redemption that shows up wherever the *imago Dei* bears the kiss of common grace. Jesus cleanses consciences and he cleanses songs one would have thought foul beyond redemption."[17]

We are not to be "conformed to this world" (Rom. 12:2), but instead to be "conformed to the image of His Son" (Rom. 8:29), that is God's Son, Jesus Christ, our Lord and Savior. When we do this, we have every assurance "that when

He appears, we will be like Him, because we will see Him just as He is" (1 John 3:2). Larry Ellis points out that God's image "is what we are to become, since it is what God designed us to be… it is an ongoing process that will be accomplished at the end of time."[18] The image of God is our purpose in life, and it gives life meaning. This is becoming what we worship, positively rather than negatively. Our ultimate goal is to be more and more like Jesus Christ, and less like any idol we might put in Christ's place. We will then exhibit the *imago Dei* as designed by God.

In the Psalms and the Old Testament prophets, we realize that those who trust in idols become like them—specifically spiritually blind, deaf, and dumb. We see the same problem today. God's original design in creating the first man is the concept of *imago Dei* or "the image of God," but idolatry turns *imago Dei* upside down. With the incarnation, though, the image of God in Christ inverts the inversion.

In the next two chapters, we will examine what the Bible, in both the Old and New Testaments, says about music's role in worship, as opposed to music becoming an idol in the place of Jesus Christ.

NOTES

[1]G.K. Beale, *We Become What We Worship: A Biblical Theology of Idolatry* (Downers Grove, IL: IVP Academic, 2008), 16.

[2]Ibid., 46.

[3]Ibid, 47.

[4]Charles H. Spurgeon, *The Treasury of David* (Peabody, MA: Hendrickson Publishers, 1988), 3:61.

[5]C.J.H. Wright, *The Mission of God* (Downers Grove, IL: InterVarsity Press, 2006), 187-188.

[6]Victor L. Wooten, *The Music Lesson: A Spiritual Search for Growth Through Music* (New York: Berkley Books, 2006), 256.

[7]James Jordan, *The Musician's Soul* (Chicago: GIA Publications, Inc., 1999), 138.

[8]Beale, *We Become What We Worship,* 307.

[9]Richard Lints, *Identity and Idolatry: The Image of God and Its Inversion* (Downers Grove, IL: InterVarsity Press, 2015).

[10]*Eerdmans Dictionary of the Bible,* "Image of God" (Grand Rapids: Eerdmans Publishing Co., 2000).

[11]Lints, *Identity and Idolatry,* 80.

[12]Ibid., 82.

[13]John Risbridger, *The Message of Worship: Celebrating the Glory of God in the Whole Life. The Bible Speaks Today,* Derek Tidball, ed. (Downers Grove, IL: InterVarsity Press, 2015), 29.

[14]Lints, 103.

[15]Ibid., 105.

[16]Risbridger, *The Message of Worship,* 137.

[17]Reggie M. Kidd, *With One Voice: Discovering Christ's Song in Our Worship* (Grand Rapids: Baker Books, 2005), 127.

[18]Larry Ellis, *Radical Worship: What Sunday Morning Can Never Give You* (Denver, CO: Adoration Publishing Co., 2014), 27.

Chapter 7

Old Testament Foundations of Music in Worship

As we move toward a prescription to restore music to its proper perspective in worship, it is essential to examine the biblical perspective on music's proper role in worship, both in the Old and New Testaments. Understanding God's framing of the music we make in worship throughout the Bible will guide us to God and away from idolatry. I am indebted to Andrew E. Hill's wonderful resource, *Baker's Handbook of Bible Lists,* for helping to identify the numerous Scripture passages related to music.[1] This chapter will focus on the biblical foundations of worship found in the Old Testament.

As I demonstrated in chapter 2, music was an integral part of worship and the Temple ministry under the reigns of King David and his son and successor, King Solomon. The role of musicians under their rule was primarily the duty of the tribe of Levi, a tradition started by David:

> Then David spoke to the chiefs of the Levites to appoint their relatives the singers, with instruments of music, harps, lyres, loud-sounding cymbals, to raise sounds of joy. (1 Chron. 15:16)

This guild of musicians involved great numbers of individuals serving not only in the area of music but also in other temple duties:

> The Levites were numbered from thirty years old and upward, and their number by census of men was 38,000. Of these, 24,000 were to oversee the work of the house of the Lord; and 6,000 *were* officers and judges, and 4,000 *were* gate-keepers, and 4,000 *were* praising the Lord with the instruments which David made for giving praise. (1 Chron. 23:3-5)

These highly trained and skillful musicians served under the strict supervision of the king:

> All these were under the direction of their father to sing in the house of the Lord, with cymbals, harps and lyres, for the service of the house of God. Asaph, Jeduthun and Heman *were* under the direction of the king. Their number who were trained in singing to the Lord, with their relatives, all who were skillful, *was* 288. (1 Chron. 25:6-7)

Most importantly, these musicians prepared their music for "the service of the house of God" (1 Chron. 25:6). In fact, when the Temple was finally built, under the reign of King Solomon, these Levitical musicians played a vital role in its dedication:

> When the priests came forth from the holy place (for all the priests who were present had sanctified themselves, without regard to divisions), and all the Levitical singers, Asaph, Heman, Jeduthun, and their sons and kinsmen, clothed in fine linen, with cymbals, harps and lyres, standing east of the altar, and with them one hundred and twenty priests blowing trumpets in unison when the trumpeters and the singers were to make themselves heard with one voice to praise and to glorify the Lord, and when they lifted up their voice accompanied by trumpets and cymbals and instruments of music, and when they praised the Lord *saying*, "*He* indeed is good for His lovingkindness is everlasting," then the house, the house of the Lord, was filled with a cloud, so that the priests could not stand to minister because of the cloud, for the glory of the Lord filled the house of God. (2 Chron. 5:11-14)

This passage not only establishes music as an effective tool in worship, but also clearly points toward the goal of music in worship: ushering in God's profound presence in a tangible way, and enhancing the declaration of God's holy Word.

As I have shown in my previous work, *The Biblical Foundations of Instrumental Music in Worship,* music was an integral part of periods of moral and spiritual revival in Israel's history, after the reigns of King David and King Solomon.[2] The word revival, in this case, is defined as times when the Israelites repented and returned to the Lord after neglect of the Law and periods of moral failure and sin often involving idolatry. One such example happened in 726 BC, when King Hezekiah repaired the house of the Lord and restored Davidic worship:

> He then stationed the Levites in the house of the Lord with cymbals, with harps and with lyres, according to the command of David and of Gad the king's seer, and of Nathan the prophet; for the command was from the Lord through His prophets. The Levites stood with the *musical* instruments of David, and the priests with the trumpets. Then Hezekiah gave the order to offer the burnt offering on the altar. When the burnt offering began, the song to the Lord also began with the trumpets, *accompanied* by the instruments of David, king of Israel. While the whole assembly worshiped, the singers also sang and the trumpets sounded; all this *continued* until the burnt offering was finished. (2 Chron. 29:25-28)

As Daniel G. Caram points out, "The revivalists always came back to the Davidic order of worship, not the Mosaic order"[3] (worship under the leadership of Moses). In every instance of revival in ancient Israel, the standard they returned to was the worship prescription of King David, with all its musical complexity. This Davidic order involved the Levites, with the singers singing and playing instruments in "song to the Lord" (2 Chron. 29:27).

Another example of the reinstitution of Davidic worship happened in 536 BC, after the restoration of Judah from Babylon and the rebuilding of the Temple, even before it was finished:

> Now when the builders had laid the foundation of the temple of the Lord, the priests stood in their apparel with trumpets, and the Levites, the sons of Asaph, with cymbals, to praise the Lord according to the directions of King David of Israel. They sang, praising and giving thanks to the Lord, *saying,* "For He is good, for His lovingkindness is upon Israel forever." And all the people shouted with a great shout when they praised the Lord because the foundation of the house of the Lord was laid. (Ezra 3:10-11)

When Nehemiah was successful in rebuilding the walls of Jerusalem a number of years later, the dedication ceremony included a reference to two great choirs and musicians "with the musical instruments of David the man of God" (Neh. 12:36). According to Kevin J. Conner, "the godly Kings of Israel who brought Israel back to the Lord always restored the order of worship that was established by David the King in the Tabernacle of David."[4] This order of worship included music in praise and worship of God, performed by musicians in service to God.

The Book of Psalms is commonly known as the songbook of ancient Israel. Hill points out that "the word *psalm* derives from the Greek *psalmos* which means 'psalm, hymn of praise…' The musical nature of the Hebrew psalms is confirmed by other words describing the compositions, especially derivatives from the roots *zämar* (sing, play, play an instrument) and *shîr* (sing)."[5]

Hill has identified ten basic literary types in Psalms, many of them music-related, that convey a wide range of emotions in worship:

1. Hymn
2. Community Lament
3. Individual Lament
4. Community Song of Thanksgiving
5. Individual Song of Thanksgiving

6. Wisdom/Torah
7. Songs of Trust
8. Royal
9. Liturgy
10. Remembrance or Storytelling.[6]

I will examine each of these types, with selected examples from the Psalms, but for a comprehensive list related to these categories, see "Directory of Psalm Literary Types" (p. 96).

Hymn

Hill describes a hymn as an "exuberant praise of God in general, a song that extols his glory and greatness as it is revealed in nature and history."[7] An excellent example of this is Psalm 95, beginning with its admonition to shout joyfully to the Lord and its testimony of God's creative power:

> O come, let us sing for joy to the Lord,
> Let us shout joyfully to the rock of our salvation.
> Let us come before His presence with thanksgiving,
> Let us shout joyfully to Him with psalms. (vv. 1-2)

The psalmist continues with a testimony of God's creative power:

> For the Lord is a great God
> And a great King above all gods,
> In whose hand are the depths of the earth,
> The peaks of the mountains are His also.
> The sea is His, for it was He who made it,
> And His hands formed the dry land. (vv. 3-5)

In response, we are encouraged to kneel in worship:

> Come, let us worship and bow down,
> Let us kneel before the Lord our Maker.
> For He is our God,
> And we are the people of His pasture and the sheep of His hand. (vv. 6-7a)

We are also encouraged to repent of our sins and not repeat the sins of our spiritual fathers:

> Today, if you would hear His voice,
> Do not harden your hearts, as at Meribah,
> As in the day of Massah in the wilderness,
> When your fathers tested Me,
> They tried Me, though they had seen My work.
> For forty years I loathed that generation,
> And said they are a people who err in their heart,
> And they do not know My ways.
> Therefore I swore in My anger,
> Truly they shall not enter into My rest. (vv. 7b-11)

Community Lament

According to Andrew Hill, a community lament is a "national expression of distress and mourning at God's apparent abandonment of his people and covenant promises."[8] Psalm 44 is representative of this literary type, with its corporate lament from God's chosen people, even though they acknowledge God's help with their forefathers and with themselves in the past:

> O God, we have heard with our ears,
> Our fathers have told us
> The work that You did in their days,
> In the days of old.
> You with Your own hand drove out the nations;
> Then You planted them;
> You afflicted the peoples,
> Then You spread them abroad.
> For by their own sword they did not possess the land,
> And their own arm did not save them,
> But Your right hand and Your arm and the light of Your presence,
> For You favored them.
>
> You are my King, O God;
> Command victories for Jacob.
> Through You we will push back our adversaries;
> Through Your name we will trample down those who rise up against us.

For I will not trust in my bow,
Nor will my sword save me.
But You have saved us from our adversaries,
And You have put to shame those who hate us.
In God we have boasted all day long,
And we will give thanks to Your name forever. Selah. (vv. 1-8)

In spite of God's faithfulness, God's chosen people complain of apparent rejection by God and reproach by neighboring nations:

Yet You have rejected us and brought us to dishonor,
And do not go out with our armies.
You cause us to turn back from the adversary;
And those who hate us have taken spoil for themselves.
You give us as sheep to be eaten
And have scattered us among the nations.
You sell Your people cheaply,
And have not profited by their sale.
You make us a reproach to our neighbors,
A scoffing and a derision to those around us.
You make us a byword among the nations,
A laughingstock among the peoples.
All day long my dishonor is before me
And my humiliation has overwhelmed me,
Because of the voice of him who reproaches and reviles,
Because of the presence of the enemy and the avenger.

All this has come upon us, but we have not forgotten You,
And we have not dealt falsely with Your covenant.
Our heart has not turned back,
And our steps have not deviated from Your way,
Yet You have crushed us in a place of jackals
And covered us with the shadow of death. (vv. 9-19)

Psalm 44 concludes with a testimony of God's omniscience and an appeal for God's help in time of need:

If we had forgotten the name of our God
Or extended our hands to a strange god,
Would not God find this out?
For He knows the secrets of the heart.
But for Your sake we are killed all day long;
We are considered as sheep to be slaughtered.
Arouse Yourself, why do You sleep, O Lord?
Awake, do not reject us forever.
Why do You hide Your face
And forget our affliction and our oppression?
For our soul has sunk down into the dust;
Our body cleaves to the earth.
Rise up, be our help,
And redeem us for the sake of Your lovingkindness. (vv. 20-26)

Individual Lament

In contrast to a community lament, an individual lament is what Hill calls "a personal expression of honest doubt about God's goodness and an appeal to God's grace and compassion for intervention in a desperate situation."[9] Psalm 56 reflects this aspect of personal lament, as the psalmist complains of the oppression of his enemies:

Be gracious to me, O God, for man has trampled upon me;
Fighting all day long he oppresses me.
My foes have trampled upon me all day long,
For they are many who fight proudly against me.
When I am afraid,
I will put my trust in You.
In God, whose word I praise,
In God I have put my trust;
I shall not be afraid.
What can mere man do to me?
All day long they distort my words;
All their thoughts are against me for evil.
They attack, they lurk,
They watch my steps,
As they have waited to take my life. (vv. 1-6)

Then the psalmist asks God for deliverance and retribution:

> Because of wickedness, cast them forth,
> In anger put down the peoples, O God!
> You have taken account of my wanderings;
> Put my tears in Your bottle.
> Are they not in Your book?
> Then my enemies will turn back in the day when I call;
> This I know, that God is for me. (vv. 7-9)

Psalm 56 ends with praise for God's deliverance:

> In God, whose word I praise,
> In the Lord, whose word I praise,
> In God I have put my trust, I shall not be afraid.
> What can man do to me?
> Your vows are binding upon me, O God;
> I will render thank offerings to You.
> For You have delivered my soul from death,
> Indeed my feet from stumbling,
> So that I may walk before God
> In the light of the living. (vv. 10-13)

Church musician and theologian Marva Dawn believes that "In general—no matter what styles of music are used—there is a lack of lament in most of the Church's worship...The use of lament forms the believers' character by providing means for worshipers to reflect upon and articulate their sense of God's hiddenness. They give the sufferer words for an urgent appeal to God, without claiming to understand the irrationality of personal circumstances."[10]

This deficiency of lament in modern worship contributes to an incomplete picture of the emotional life of the Christian believer, one that is devoid of questioning God in times of trial. We need to have a more balanced approach to worship that includes lament. When we consider the abundance of psalms that are identified as lament (see Appendix 2, p. 96) compared to the other literary types, it does not line up with the general lack of that expression in the church's worship.

Community Song of Thanksgiving

Andrew Hill explains that a community song of thanksgiving "expands the vow of praise found at the end of many laments." It is "a corporate praise response to God in gratitude for a specific act of deliverance experienced by the nation."[11] Psalm 124 is representative of this type, as the people of Israel express their gratitude to God for God's deliverance from their enemies:

> "Had it not been the Lord who was on our side,"
> Let Israel now say,
> "Had it not been the Lord who was on our side
> When men rose up against us,
> Then they would have swallowed us alive,
> When their anger was kindled against us;
> Then the waters would have engulfed us,
> The stream would have swept over our soul;
>
> Then the raging waters would have swept over our soul."
> Blessed be the Lord,
> Who has not given us to be torn by their teeth.
> Our soul has escaped as a bird out of the snare of the trapper;
> The snare is broken and we have escaped.
> Our help is in the name of the Lord,
> Who made heaven and earth.

Individual Song of Thanksgiving

Just as there are community and individual laments, there are also community and individual songs of thanksgiving. Hill labels an individual song of thanksgiving as a "personal confession of gratitude and praise for God's providential intervention in a time of need, delivering the suppliant from a specific trial, distress, or illness."[12] Psalm 116 is an excellent example of this literary type, with its heartfelt expression of gratitude to God for divine provision of salvation and deliverance from death. The psalmist first declares his love and devotion to the Lord because of answered prayer:

> I love the Lord, because He hears
> My voice and my supplications.
> Because He has inclined His ear to me,
> Therefore I shall call upon Him as long as I live.
> The cords of death encompassed me

And the terrors of Sheol came upon me;
I found distress and sorrow.
Then I called upon the name of the Lord:
"O Lord, I beseech You, save my life!" (vv. 1-4)

This declaration of love and devotion to God is followed by thanksgiving for salvation and deliverance, and confession that God alone is trustworthy—not man:

Gracious is the Lord, and righteous;
Yes, our God is compassionate.
The Lord preserves the simple;
I was brought low, and He saved me.
Return to your rest, O my soul,
For the Lord has dealt bountifully with you.
For You have rescued my soul from death,
My eyes from tears,
My feet from stumbling.
I shall walk before the Lord
In the land of the living.
I believed when I said,
"I am greatly afflicted."
I said in my alarm,
"All men are liars." (vv. 5-11)

The psalm ends with praise, in gratitude for God's goodness:

What shall I render to the Lord
For all His benefits toward me?
I shall lift up the cup of salvation
And call upon the name of the Lord.
I shall pay my vows to the Lord,
Oh may it be in the presence of all His people.
Precious in the sight of the Lord
Is the death of His godly ones.
O Lord, surely I am Your servant,
I am Your servant, the son of Your handmaid,
You have loosed my bonds.
To You I shall offer a sacrifice of thanksgiving,

And call upon the name of the Lord.
I shall pay my vows to the Lord,
Oh may it be in the presence of all His people,
In the courts of the Lord's house,
In the midst of you, O Jerusalem.
Praise the Lord! (vv. 12-19)

Wisdom/Torah

Hill classifies the Wisdom/Torah psalms as "essentially meditations on the righteous life, instruction in the fear of the Lord, and admonitions to good conduct rooted in obedience to the Torah, sometimes contrasting the righteous and the wicked."[13] A very familiar and appropriate example is Psalm 1 (the text used at my ordination service). The words of this psalm summarize the aspirations of persons entering ministry, but really anyone who wants to live in a way that honors the Lord:

How blessed is the man who does not walk in the counsel of the wicked,
Nor stand in the path of sinners,
Nor sit in the seat of scoffers!
But his delight is in the law of the Lord,
And in His law he meditates day and night.
He will be like a tree firmly planted by streams of water,
Which yields its fruit in its season
And its leaf does not wither;
And in whatever he does, he prospers. (vv. 1-3)

The psalmist then contrasts the righteous servant with the plight of the wicked:

The wicked are not so,
But they are like chaff which the wind drives away.
Therefore the wicked will not stand in the judgment,
Nor sinners in the assembly of the righteous.
For the Lord knows the way of the righteous,
But the way of the wicked will perish. (vv. 4-6)

Songs of Trust

Hill tells us that songs of trust "emphasize the nearness of God, his compassion, and saving power."[14] This literary type is exhibited in Psalm 11, with its pledge to take refuge in the Lord and God's assurance of protection for the righteous, but judgment on the wicked:

In the Lord I take refuge;
How can you say to my soul, "Flee as a bird to your mountain;
For, behold, the wicked bend the bow,
They make ready their arrow upon the string
To shoot in darkness at the upright in heart.
If the foundations are destroyed,
What can the righteous do?"

The Lord is in His holy temple; the Lord's throne is in heaven;
His eyes behold, His eyelids test the sons of men.
The Lord tests the righteous and the wicked,
And the one who loves violence His soul hates.
Upon the wicked He will rain snares;
Fire and brimstone and burning wind will be the portion of their cup.
For the Lord is righteous, He loves righteousness;
The upright will behold His face.

Royal

Hill defines the royal psalm as an "exaltation of the Israelite king and/or the Davidic covenant of kingship, emphasizing the divine appointment and protection of the Hebrew king."[15] Psalm 2 demonstrates this literary type, which also clearly anticipates the rule of God's Son and our Messiah:

Why are the nations in an uproar
And the peoples devising a vain thing?
The kings of the earth take their stand
And the rulers take counsel together
Against the Lord and against His Anointed, saying,
"Let us tear their fetters apart
And cast away their cords from us!"

He who sits in the heavens laughs,
The Lord scoffs at them.
Then He will speak to them in His anger
And terrify them in His fury, saying,
"But as for Me, I have installed My King
Upon Zion, My holy mountain."

"I will surely tell of the decree of the Lord:
He said to Me, 'You are My Son,
Today I have begotten You.
'Ask of Me, and I will surely give the nations as Your inheritance,
And the very ends of the earth as Your possession.
'You shall break them with a rod of iron,
You shall shatter them like earthenware.'" (vv. 1-9)

Psalm 2 ends with a fervent appeal for the rulers of this world to pay homage to the Son, the King of kings:

Now therefore, O kings, show discernment;
Take warning, O judges of the earth.
Worship the Lord with reverence
And rejoice with trembling.
Do homage to the Son, that He not become angry, and you perish in the way,
For His wrath may soon be kindled.
How blessed are all who take refuge in Him! (vv. 10-12)

Liturgy

In liturgy psalms Hill finds "reflections on aspects of ancient Hebrew worship and ritual, especially formal entrance to the temple and covenant renewal ceremonies."[16] We see this literary type in Psalm 15, with its reference to God's tent and God's holy hill, and the litany of righteous traits required for entrance:

O Lord, who may abide in Your tent?
Who may dwell on Your holy hill?
He who walks with integrity, and works righteousness,
And speaks truth in his heart.
He does not slander with his tongue,
Nor does evil to his neighbor,
Nor takes up a reproach against his friend;
In whose eyes a reprobate is despised,
But who honors those who fear the Lord;
He swears to his own hurt and does not change;
He does not put out his money at interest,
Nor does he take a bribe against the innocent.
He who does these things will never be shaken.

Remembrance/Storytelling

Finally, a remembrance or storytelling psalm is what Hill calls a "recitation of Yahweh's past redemptive acts on behalf of Israel, presented as a confession of faith."[17] Psalms of this type are naturally longer, such as Psalm 135, with its mention of God's choice of Jacob and Israel, God's deliverance of the Israelites from Egypt, and God's gift and blessing of the Promised Land and the Holy City, Jerusalem:

> Praise the Lord!
> Praise the name of the Lord;
> Praise Him, O servants of the Lord,
> You who stand in the house of the Lord,
> In the courts of the house of our God!
> Praise the Lord, for the Lord is good;
> Sing praises to His name, for it is lovely.
> For the Lord has chosen Jacob for Himself,
> Israel for His own possession.
>
> For I know that the Lord is great
> And that our Lord is above all gods.
> Whatever the Lord pleases, He does,
> In heaven and in earth, in the seas and in all deeps.
> He causes the vapors to ascend from the ends of the earth;
> Who makes lightnings for the rain,
> Who brings forth the wind from His treasuries.
>
> He smote the firstborn of Egypt,
> Both of man and beast.
> He sent signs and wonders into your midst, O Egypt,
> Upon Pharaoh and all his servants.
> He smote many nations
> And slew mighty kings,
> Sihon, king of the Amorites,
> And Og, king of Bashan,
> And all the kingdoms of Canaan;
> And He gave their land as a heritage,
> A heritage to Israel His people.
> Your name, O Lord, is everlasting,
> Your remembrance, O Lord, throughout all generations.

For the Lord will judge His people
And will have compassion on His servants. (vv. 1-14)

The psalmist then condemns the idolatry of the nations, in all its foolishness:

The idols of the nations are but silver and gold,
The work of man's hands.
They have mouths, but they do not speak;
They have eyes, but they do not see;
They have ears, but they do not hear,
Nor is there any breath at all in their mouths.
Those who make them will be like them,
Yes, everyone who trusts in them. (vv. 15-18)

Finally, Psalm 135 ends with repeated blessing, directed to the Lord:

O house of Israel, bless the Lord;
O house of Aaron, bless the Lord;
O house of Levi, bless the Lord;
You who revere the Lord, bless the Lord.
Blessed be the Lord from Zion,
Who dwells in Jerusalem.
Praise the Lord! (vv. 19-21)

Remembrance and storytelling are very biblical practices, as evidenced in both the Old and New Testaments. Both the Passover and the Lord's Supper are times of remembrance, recalling the deliverance of the Israelites from Egypt and the sacrifice of Jesus on the cross for our sins. Jesus himself was the master storyteller, often using parables in his teaching throughout the Gospels.

All of these literary types are poetic forms, lending themselves to be sung in worship and reflecting the differing responses to God of praise, lament, thanksgiving, trust, and faith. Sigmund Mowinckel concludes: "...in the psalms the human heart has found its own counterpart at all times, in sorrow and in happiness, as an individual and as a member of God's people."[18] David Taylor reminds us that "During the early centuries of the church, the singing of the psalms represented the superlative vehicle for unified praise."[19] The Book of Psalms stands as the most loved and utilized book in the Old Testament. Anthem settings of the Psalms are especially moving and effective in worship, as there is nothing more powerful than singing God's Word.

The Psalms are an important link between the two Testaments, according to Hill, as "evidenced by the extensive appeal to the Psalter by the New Testament writers. The New Testament contains more than four hundred quotations and allusions to the Psalms, second only to the book of Isaiah."[20] In addition, "the tradition of singing the Psalms as part of worship in the early church is confirmed by the writings of the ante-Nicene church fathers (before the Council of Nicea, AD 325)."[21] Examples of those church fathers include Clement of Alexandria, Origin, and Tertullian, all of whom spoke about singing psalms and hymns in early Christian worship. The continued singing of psalms is found in a number of churches today, but completely neglected by many churches.

Music in the Old Testament practice of worship is rooted in the institution of King David and continued through his royal successors. The Psalms are an exhaustive resource for Old Testament worship, and continue to be used in Christian worship today. The Psalter is therefore an important bridge between the two testamental periods.

NOTES

[1]Andrew E. Hill, *Baker's Handbook of Bible Lists* (Grand Rapids: Baker Books, 1981).

[2]Brian L. Hedrick, *The Biblical Foundations of Instrumental Music in Worship: Four Pillars* (Denver, CO: Outskirts Press, 2009), 34.

[3]Daniel G. Caram, *Tabernacle of David* (Longwood, FL: Xulon Press, 2003), 98.

[4]Kevin J. Conner, *The Tabernacle of David* (Portland, OR: City Bible Publishing, 1989), 145.

[5]Andrew E. Hill, *Enter His Courts with Praise! Old Testament Worship for the New Testament Church* (Grand Rapids: Baker Books, 1996), 201.

[6]Ibid., 197-199

[7]Ibid., 197.

[8]Ibid., 198.

[9]Ibid.

[10]Marva Dawn, *Reaching Out without Dumbing Down: A Theology of Worship for the Turn-of-the-Century Culture* (Grand Rapids: Eerdmans Publishing Co., 1995), 176.

[11]Hill, *Enter His Courts with Praise!,* 198.

[12]Ibid.

[13]Ibid., 199.

[14]Ibid.

[15]Ibid.

[16]Ibid.

[17]Ibid.

[18]Sigmund Mowinckel, *The Psalms in Israel's Worship* (Grand Rapids: Eerdmans Publishing Co., 2004), 1.

[19]W. David Taylor, *Glimpses of the New Creation: Worship and the Formative Power of the Arts* (Grand Rapids: Eerdmans Publishing Co., 2019), 76.

[20]Hill, *Enter His Courts with Praise!,* 207.

[21]Ibid.

Chapter 8

New Testament Foundations of Music in Worship

Music in the Christian worship of the New Testament and the early church was not as prevalent as worship in the Old Testament, due to intense persecution and the clandestine nature of worship gatherings. Despite those circumstances, there are numerous Scripture references to music in the New Testament. Hymn singing was associated with the Lord's Supper, from the beginning of the institution with Jesus and the disciples: "After singing a hymn, they went out to the Mount of Olives" (Matt. 26:30, Mark 14:26). We do not know exactly what the disciples sang with Jesus that night, but many scholars believe it was one of the "Hallel" psalms (113–118). These psalms were typically sung at the slaying of the Paschal lamb, a Passover practice and tradition that foreshadowed the death of Jesus Christ as the Lamb of God.

Two early examples of New Testament songs appear in the opening chapter of Luke's gospel. Mary, the mother of Jesus, responded with a joyous song of praise to God, in reply to Elizabeth's prophetic greeting:

> My soul exalts the Lord,
> And my spirit has rejoiced in God my Savior.
> For He has had regard for the humble state of His bondslave;
> For behold, from this time on all generations will count me blessed.
> For the Mighty One has done great things for me;
> And holy is His name.
> And His mercy is upon generation after generation
> Toward those who fear Him.
> He has done mighty deeds with His arm;
> He has scattered *those who were* proud in the thoughts of their heart.
> He has brought down rulers from *their* thrones,
> And has exalted those who were humble.
> He has filled the hungry with good things;
> And sent away the rich empty-handed.
> He has given help to Israel His servant,
> In remembrance of His mercy,
> As He spoke to our fathers,
> To Abraham and his descendants forever. (1:46-55)

After the return of his speech, Zechariah verified his son's name and in a song of blessing to God, prophesied about his son's role in preparing the way for the Savior:

> Blessed *be* the Lord God of Israel,
> For He has visited us and accomplished redemption for His people,
> And has raised up a horn of salvation for us
> In the house of David His servant—
> As He spoke by the mouth of His holy prophets from of old—
> Salvation from our enemies,
> And from the hand of all who hate us;
> To show mercy toward our fathers,
> And to remember His holy covenant,
> The oath which He swore to Abraham our father,
> To grant us that we, being rescued from the hand of our enemies,
> Might serve Him without fear,
> In holiness and righteousness before Him all our days.
> And you, child, will be called the prophet of the Most High;
> For you will go on before the Lord to prepare His ways;
> To give to His people *the* knowledge of salvation
> By the forgiveness of their sins,
> Because of the tender mercy of our God,
> With which the Sunrise from on high will visit us,
> To shine upon those who sit in darkness and the shadow of death,
> To guide our feet into the way of peace. (1:68-79)

Both the Song of Mary (the *Magnificat*) and the Song of Zechariah (the *Benedictus*) are commonly used canticles in Christian worship, which Susan J. White defines as "biblical texts other than the Psalms that are set to music for singing."[1] Paul S. Jones says of canticles:

> Like the Old Testament psalms, these biblical songs, recorded in written form, were passed on by oral tradition from priests to people and parents to children… canticles typically rehearse the attributes of God and his mighty acts on behalf of his people—specifically his acts of *creation* and *redemption.* They give glory to God and manifest a spirit of joy and thankfulness for his work and deliverance.[2]

Mary's Song closely resembles Hannah's Song in the first chapter of 1 Samuel. Hannah breaks into a song of thanksgiving after she dedicates her son, Samuel, to the Lord. Both Hannah's Song and Mary's Song begin with similar expressions of praise: "My heart exults in the Lord; my horn is exalted in the Lord" (1 Sam. 2:1) and "My soul exalts the Lord, and my spirit has rejoiced in God my Savior" (Luke 1:46-47). Both songs go on to extol the Lord and the Lord's marvelous and mighty deeds among the nations. Mary seems to have surely known and been influenced by Hannah's Song, which was sung a thousand years earlier.

Both of the New Testament canticles are taken from the Book of Luke. Taylor observes: "Like characters in a musical theatre production, the protagonists of Luke's Gospel find mere speech insufficient to the task of expressing the astonishing events that occur to them. The Virgin Mary breaks out in song in response to Elizabeth's benediction. Zechariah sings his way out of silence at the pronouncement of his son's name."[3] Taylor then adds a reference to two other familiar canticles in the Book of Luke: "The angel choir sings of God's fantastic glory (Luke 2:14), while Simeon erupts in verse at the sight of the Christ child (Luke 2:29-32)."[4]

Biblical evidence of worship through song continues in the early church, as evidenced in the Acts of the Apostles. In spite of their dire circumstances, Paul and Silas were openly worshiping God while in prison: "But about midnight Paul and Silas were praying and singing hymns of praise to God, and the prisoners were listening to them" (Acts 16:25). This passage not only reminds us of the power of praise, as Paul and Silas were immediately set free from their bonds, but also helps us remember that music can be used powerfully in worship settings outside of church services—even in prison!

The Apostle Paul not only practiced worship through singing, but also encouraged others to do the same. In numerous passages he encouraged the early church to use psalms and hymns and spiritual songs in praise to the Lord, including Romans 15:9, 1 Corinthians 14:26, and most notably in these passages from his letters to the Ephesians and the Colossians:

> Speaking to one another in psalms and hymns and spiritual songs, singing and making melody with your heart to the Lord. (Eph. 5:19).

> Let the word of Christ richly dwell within you, with all wisdom teaching and admonishing one another with psalms *and* hymns *and* spiritual songs, singing with thankfulness in your hearts to God. (Col. 3:16)

Not only do these passages provide a link to Old Testament worship, through the mention of psalms, but they also demonstrate a variety in musical expressions, both including "psalms *and* hymns *and* spiritual songs." There are a variety of opinions on exactly what these terms might mean (besides the obvious reference to the Psalms), but at the least it implies that there is more than one way and one style acceptable in Christian worship. There is also a clear implication that our worship can be both vertical and horizontal.

Vertical worship is directed specifically to God: "singing and making melody in your heart to the Lord" and "singing with thankfulness in your hearts to God." But worship can also be horizontal, as we encourage one another in song: "speaking to one another in psalms and hymns and spiritual songs" and "teaching and admonishing one another with psalms *and* hymns *and* spiritual songs." This horizontal aspect of worship fulfills a pedagogical function, as believers teach and encourage one another in Christian fellowship and song.

The supreme example of vertical worship is found in the Book of Revelation. Depicting heavenly worship, in John's revelation of Jesus Christ, the four living creatures and the twenty-four elders sing a new song of worship to the Lamb, one of "five hymns sung by heavenly choirs"[5] in Revelation 4 and 5 (4:6b-9, 11; 5:9-10, 12, 13):

> When He had taken the book, the four living creatures and the twenty-four elders fell down before the Lamb, each one holding a harp and golden bowls full of incense, which are the prayers of the saints. And they sang a new song, saying, "Worthy are You to take the book and to break its seals; for You were slain, and purchased for God with Your blood *men* from every tribe and tongue and people and nation. You have made them *to be* a kingdom and priests to our God; and they will reign upon the earth." (5:8-10)

As John Risbridger suggests, "this heavenly worship provides a powerful model to inspire and shape our worship on earth."[6] Interpreting Scripture in light of Scripture, we remember Jesus' words in the Lord's Prayer: "Your kingdom come, Your will be done, on earth as it is in heaven" (Matt. 6:10). Heavenly worship, as depicted in Revelation, should influence our worship here on earth. It should be Christ-centered, rich and full, inspiring awe-filled passionate worship.

The use of music in worship is prevalent in both the Old and New Testaments. It was instituted formally by King David, performed by the Levites, and carried on in Old Testament worship by King Solomon and King Hezekiah and in other times of revival in temple worship, dedication, and commitment to the Lord. In the New Testament, music was linked to the Lord's Supper by Jesus, practiced by Jesus' mother, Mary, in praise for God's favor, and used in the prophetic blessing of God by Zechariah, John the Baptist's father. Paul and Silas sang a hymn of praise to God, not in a worship service, but in prison, with amazing results. Paul encourages us to use psalms and hymns and spiritual songs in worship throughout his letters, and John gives us a glimpse of music in heavenly worship of the Lamb of God in his Book of Revelation.

Music is therefore clearly established as a vital part of authentic worship, in both the Old and New Testaments, from the time of King David through the glimpse of heavenly worship depicted in The Revelation to John. The key to avoiding musical idolatry is to follow the biblical precedent and practices of worship. With this biblical model firmly established, we move on to a prescription to restore music to its proper place.

NOTES

[1]Susan J. White, *Foundations of Christian Worship* (Louisville, KY: Westminster John Knox Press, 2006), 52.

[2]Paul S. Jones, *Singing and Making Music: Issues in Church Music Today* (Phillipsburg, NJ: P&R Publishing Co., 2006), 102.

[3]W. David Taylor, *Glimpses of the New Creation: Worship and the Formative Power of the Arts* (Grand Rapids: Eerdmans Publishing Co., 2019), 75.

[4]Ibid.

[5]Allen P. Ross, *Recalling the Hope of Glory: Biblical Worship from the Garden to the New Creation* (Grand Rapids: Kregel Publications, 2006), 481.

[6]John Risbridger, *The Message of Worship: Celebrating the Glory of God in the Whole Life. The Bible Speaks Today*, Derek Tidball, ed. (Downers Grove, IL: InterVarsity Press, 2015), 87.

Chapter 9

Restoring Music to Its Proper Biblical Place

In this final chapter I will propose a plan for restoring music to its proper biblical place, not as an idol, but as a tool and creative offering to God for God's glory. Author Con Campbell writes, "We need to affirm the wonder and beauty of art [music], but also teach that it is not god."[1]

The first step in restoring music to its proper biblical place is realizing the error of our ways. Even the disciple whom Jesus loved, the Apostle John, was found guilty of misplaced worship. In Revelation 22, John is shown by an angel "the things which must soon take place" (v. 6). Then John "fell down to worship at the feet of the angel who showed (him) these things" (v. 8). The angel quickly admonished him, saying "Do not do that. I am a fellow servant of yours and of your brethren the prophets and of those who heed the words of this book. Worship God" (v. 9).

None of us are immune to the subtleties of idolatry. If John, the beloved disciple, could mistakenly direct his worship to some person or some thing delivering God's message, we are surely prone to this error also. This misplaced devotion can be directed toward a pastor who effectively preaches God's Word, a gifted musician who leads us in worship, or the music itself that carries the message from God or our devotion to God. We must remember the admonishment of the angel to John: "Do not do that... Worship God!"[2]

Worship leaders particularly need to realize that it is very easy to foster this misplaced devotion in worship services without even realizing what we have done. Stephen Miller cautions:

> It is the job of worship leaders to raise the affections of the people we lead to the highest possible height with the truth of the worthiness of God in our songs. And yet, while emotions are helpful handmaids of worship, the emotional and even sensual nature of music can make it difficult to know whether we are raising the affection of our hearers with the truth or simply the thrill of the song. We may go for the jugular and completely fail to exalt the character, holiness, and majesty of God. The music becomes self-serving.[3]

A good example of this misplaced devotion is the story behind "The Heart of Worship," a contemporary worship song, written by Matt Redman in the late 1990s. It was birthed out of a situation at the church he was serving at the time, Soul

Survivor in Watford, England, outside London. It was a large church, with a younger congregation and cutting-edge worship music that was drawing large crowds. The pastor felt that despite all of that apparent success, however, there was still something missing. He felt that the crowd was drawn to the music, not necessarily to worshiping God. Consequently, the church leaders eliminated the band and turned off the sound system, leaving the congregation to worship with only their unaccompanied voices and without the use of sound reinforcement. The song speaks of stripping everything away and getting back to the heart of worship, which is all about Jesus:

> When the music fades
> And all is stripped away
> And I simply come
> Longing just to bring
> Something that's of worth
> That will bless Your heart
>
> I'll bring You more than a song
> For a song in itself
> Is not what You have required.
> You search much deeper within
> Through the way things appear
> You're looking into my heart
>
> I'm coming back to the heart of worship
> And it's all about You, it's all about You, Jesus.
> I'm sorry, Lord, for the thing I've made it
> It's all about You, Jesus.[4]

This church and song provide a classic example of an instance where music had become an idol. Church leaders took drastic measures to get their worship practices back in proper perspective. They systematically "stripped away" everything the congregation had taken pride in, leaving only their simple, unaccompanied devotion to Christ. Eventually, the church restored the band and the sound system to accompany their singing. It was a fruitful experience for the congregation that was effective in emphasizing the true object of worship—God and God alone. I am not suggesting that all churches consider stripping away all musical accompaniment and sound reinforcement, but some drastic measures may need to be taken to awaken our congregations to the fact that music may have moved from serving as a tool in worship to being the object of worship.

With this real temptation to musical idolatry, some Christians may wonder if we should just avoid music altogether. Swiss reformer Huldriech Zwingli (1484–1531) surely felt that way. Jeremy S. Begbie characterizes the reformer as having "an overplayed fear of anything that might imply an idolatry of music."[5] Among Zwingli's reforms was the total elimination of music from worship, although he was an accomplished musician himself. His attitude was that "music, bound up as it is so closely with physical things, is regarded at best irrelevant and at worst dangerous, tugging us away from the more real, nonsensory 'spiritual' realities."[6] These drastic measures from the Swiss reformer seem rather harsh in today's music-rich worship environment. Begbie asks us to consider that "the lasting antidote to idolatry is not to spurn what is God-created but to do all in one's power to turn it to the praise of God, to release it to sing the goodness of the Creator."[7] If music is truly used to bring glory to God and not humans, then it is a good and acceptable practice. Campbell insists that "We have no business telling an artist that they must quit their art if they want to be a Christian. No, their gift is from Christ; who are we to take that away? The secret is not to pit art and Christ against one another in such a way that only one will be left standing. They are in competition only if art is occupying Christ's position as number one. Once he is recognized as Lord, art will find its place. *Its place is under him.*"[8]

We also need a call for pastors to take ownership of the worship expression in their congregations. Lead pastors are often very busy with their many duties, including sermon preparation, administration, and ministering to the needs of the congregation. John Risbridger explains:

> In such a world the easy option is simply to hand the worship life of the church over to a team of highly talented musicians (of whom many are deeply spiritual people) as if it were a specialized ministry for musical people. Certainly the gifts of such people must be honored and their spiritual leadership given space to flourish, but if worship is the sign and goal of salvation and the proper response to it, then pastors must see that the nurturing of a worshipping community lies at the heart of their responsibilities.[9]

Lead pastors must remember that they are worshipers also. In fact, they are the lead-worshipers, setting an example to the congregation of how they should appropriately respond in worship. What pastors preach each week should be reflected in all other parts of congregational worship, and lead pastors need to take ownership of all of worship—not just the sermon. Pastors need to work in partnership with their worship leaders, so that the entire expression of worship is a cohesive whole.

This need may be addressed practically by having regular programming meetings for worship, preferably with the lead pastor present. There must be a constant dialogue between those who plan worship, outside of the sermon, and the pastor who preaches the sermon. These programming meetings should address immediate plans for the worship experience and also long-range plans, knowing that change is inevitable, as they receive direction from the lead pastor. These meetings can also be used to evaluate worship after the fact, celebrating meaningful worship experiences or discussing how to correct worship that did not quite meet expectations.

As pastors and worship leaders work together on the cohesive expression of worship, it must be *Christocentric* (having Christ as its center). Timothy Keller rightly points out that:

> Idolatry is not just a failure to obey God, it is a setting of the whole heart on something besides God. This cannot be remedied only by repenting that you have an idol, or using willpower to try to live differently. Turning from idols is not less than those two things, but it is also far more. "Setting the mind and heart on things above" where "your life is hid with Christ in God" (Col. 3:1-3) means appreciation, rejoicing, and resting in what Jesus has done for you. It entails joyful worship, a sense of God's reality in prayer. Jesus must become more beautiful to your imagination, more attractive to your heart, than your idol. That is what will replace your counterfeit gods. If you uproot the idol and fail to "plant" the love of Christ in its place, the idol will grow back.[10]

This relapse is inevitable unless our worship is truly Christ-centered.

What this mindset means, according to Harold Best, is "Faith rules over works, maker over handiwork, revelation over creation, and Creator over all. It is God who is both means and end, alpha and omega, author and finisher. Knowing this and living it out rescues both us and our art from error, misuse, and above all, idolatry."[11] God has created people to be creative creatures, but God is the only Creator—and worthy of worship!

Citing Matthew 10:39, D.A. Carson writes, "in the same way that according to Jesus, you cannot find yourself until you lose yourself, so also you cannot find excellent corporate worship until you stop trying to find excellent corporate worship and pursue God Himself."[12] As a start, we should do as the 1976 chorus by Bruce Ballinger, "We Have Come Into His House," says: "Let's forget about ourselves, and magnify the Lord, and worship Him."[13]

Once we realize and are convicted that music has taken the place of supreme devotion, reserved for God, we must do everything possible to "set the mind on the things above." This commitment to repentance can take the form of many proven spiritual practices, for example:

- daily time studying God's Word and communing with God in prayer
- sitting under the teaching of a faithful, godly pastor in the context of corporate worship
- studying God's Word in the fellowship of other Christians
- expanding our expression of devotion by serving in ministries in addition to the ministry of music

These practices are particularly important for those who are called to full-time or part-time vocational music ministry, but also for anyone called to worship leadership, paid or unpaid. Our personal devotion to Christ must take precedence over our devotion to our ministry duties, and our ministry duties must never take the place of our devotion to Christ. The one must not be mistaken for the other.

Speaking from personal experience, the longer I serve in ministry (thirty-five years as of this writing), the more I treasure and depend on my personal time with the Lord each day. When I first began in ministry, my personal devotion time was simple *drudgery.* So many other activities seemed to squeeze it out. Through years of *discipline* and perseverance, I am now at a time when I rarely miss a day in God's Word and prayer, and it has become a daily *delight.* This commitment has become an indispensable practice for consistent vocational ministry. I simply could not survive without it.

Frank Page and Lavon Gray, in their book, *Hungry for Worship,* provide a helpful evaluation tool for persons serving in Christian worship ministry, highlighting four hard questions that Christian musicians must ask themselves, but may find they do not like the answers:

1. Am I more passionate about music than I am about the God of the Ages?
2. Do I spend as much time in prayer and Bible study as I do on rehearsing and leading?
3. Is my role in the worship service a performance opportunity or a chance to lead people to the throne of God?
4. If the music was gone, how strong would my faith commitment be?[14]

They continue, "As Christian musicians we can get so involved in perfecting the tool that we lose sight of what the tool was designed to do in the first place."[15] So what was that tool designed to do in the first place?

I propose that one of music's roles is to assist in shaping an environment where sinful humans can meet a holy God in awe-filled worship. Marva Dawn suggests that "this sense of God's greatness, fullness, and mystery is often missing in modern worship. Certainly the course of time gives place for all kinds of worship moods and attitudes, for God is an infinitely diverse God." Dawn is "disturbed that the awesomeness of God is repeatedly swallowed up by coziness. Not only the Church but God himself is dumbed down, made too small, trivialized."[16] What then is the answer to this "dumbing down" of worship? Church worship leaders must acknowledge the goal of creating an atmosphere where worshipers can encounter a holy God in awe-filled worship, doing all they can to promote this ideal, and avoiding everything that detracts from it.

Isaiah 6 gives us a perfect model for this encounter. The passage begins, "In the year of King Uzziah's death I saw the Lord sitting on a throne, lofty and exalted, with the train of His robe filling the temple" (v. 1). As Isaiah took in this vision, his first response was one of unworthiness. As he stood before a holy God, his first impression was an acute awareness of his innate sinfulness. Isaiah could only confess humbly, "I am a man of unclean lips" (v. 5). Often in worship we are missing a sense of awe of almighty God, which should lead us to a sense of unworthiness and humility. All else will pale in comparison and be exposed as idols.

Thankfully, we not only serve a holy God, but also a God who stands ready to cleanse and forgive. A.W. Tozer explains it this way: "Isaiah's lips, symbolic of all his nature, were purified by fire. God could then say to him, 'Thine iniquity is taken away' (Isa. 6:7). That is how the amazed and pained Isaiah could genuinely come to a sense of restored moral innocence. That is how he instantly found that he was ready for worship and that he was also ready and anxious for service in the will of God."[17] This profound encounter must be restored to our worship services. Tozer prays, "May God show us a vision of ourselves that will disvalue us to the point of total devaluation. From there He can raise us up to worship Him and to praise Him and to witness."[18]

This worship that we express to God needs therefore to be centered more on what God has done for us, rather than on what we have done for God. We need to minimize the use of songs that simply express nothing but what Risbridger calls "extravagant claims of devotion to God"[19] and strengthen our focus on proclaiming the excellencies of the goodness of God that might provoke such devotion.[20] When we gather for worship each week, our story needs to be God's story—not our own.

Robert E. Webber explores the concept that worship proclaims what God has done for us, or God's story, in his book, *Ancient-Future Worship.*[21] "Worship is not a program. Nor is worship about *me.* Worship is a narrative—God's narrative of the world from its beginning to end. How will the world know its own story unless we do that story in public worship?"[22] If non-Christians were to walk into our worship services, and later were asked to describe Christianity, based strictly on what they observed in our songs, would they get a complete picture of the God we worship, or would they just observe us singing songs of devotion to an unnamed, undefined deity?

Webber maintains that "when worship fails to proclaim, sing, and enact ... the Good News that God not only saves sinners but also narrates the whole world, it is not only worship that becomes corrupted by culture," but it is worship that has "lost its way" and "the fullness of the gospel, the story which worship does, has been lost."[23] We must strive toward the concept, Webber suggests, that "remembers the past"[24] and "anticipates the future."[25] Biblical and historical worship does not focus on the individual in worship. Rather, it focuses on God through remembering God's saving acts through history.

The premise of remembrance in worship is supported by numerous passages in both the Old and New Testaments, and confirmed by the simple act of looking up the word "remember" in a Bible concordance. Through the numerous references, spread throughout Scripture, we see that God's people are called repeatedly to remember God's saving acts.

Another way to think of worship, as expressed in Webber's book, *Worship Old and New*, is to consider the fundamental issues of content, structure, and style. He maintains that "the primary factor in worship concerns not the structure, not the style, but the content."[26] The content of our worship should never change. "For worship to be biblical and Christian, the story of God's redemption and salvation must be its content. Otherwise it ceases to be Christian worship. For it is the content of worship—the Gospel—that makes worship uniquely and distinctly Christian."[27]

The other two ways of thinking about worship, structure and style, are not as important as the content of our worship. Structure can change from church to church and even from week to week, but should ideally include the historically established elements of Gathering, Word, Table, and Sending. Style is ever changing and is the least important of these three ways of thinking about worship, both from a biblical and historical frame of reference (but regrettably is where most of the conflict is found in churches).

One of my favorite books on worship is Sally Morgenthaler's *Worship Evangelism*.[28] This book with its timeless message was written in 1995, and the objective of the book was bringing Baby Boomers (born 1946–1964) back to church worship services and attracting Baby Busters (born 1965–1979, also known as Generation X) to church worship services. Despite its generational application, its message is still relevant today—especially in relation to the subject of this book. In chapter 5 of her book, Morgenthaler identifies four "essentials" for worship evangelism,[29] but these could easily apply to worship in general:

1. Nearness—a Sense of God's Presence
2. Knowledge—Worship Centered on Christ
3. Vulnerability—Opening Up to God
4. Interaction—Participating in a Relationship with God and Others

These four essentials serve as an effective summary of the principles for putting music back in its proper place in worship.

Nearness relates to promoting a sense of awe in worship, a point illustrated earlier in this chapter, as we consider Isaiah's profound encounter with a holy God, as described in Isaiah 6. When contemplating this first essential, Morgenthaler asks the question, "Who is ultimately responsible for the experience of God's presence in worship, the worshiper or God?"[30] Morgenthaler maintains that "the first and most basic concept Scripture gives us about God's manifest presence is that God is already there waiting for us. In other words, God's nearness is not something we 'bring down,' 'whip up,' or otherwise manipulate. God's presence is always something we 'come into.'"[31] This concept reminds us that music must be used only to point the worshiper to the already existing, manifest presence of God in our worship services. To quote C.S. Lewis, "It is in the process of being worshipped that God communicates His presence to men."[32]

Knowledge is the second essential, specifically worship centered on Christ. This is the all-important content of our worship, the one aspect of worship that should be unchanging. For many churches, the style of worship is ever changing, and the structure of worship may change in subtle ways. The content of our worship should never change, however. It is always the story of God's redemption and salvation, which has been accomplished for us through the finished work of Jesus Christ on the cross. The practical application of this essential is pointed out by Morgenthaler: "God's character as revealed by the Word of God must be an integral part of our services."[33] In other words, "Knowing *who* it is we worship is the second essential for worship."[34]

Vulnerability is specifically opening up to God. Morgenthaler points out that this is related to an "almost insatiable craving for... authenticity"[35] in worship by the average worshiper. Individuals must come to worship, knowing they are free to communicate a variety of emotions, including those expressed in the psalms of lament (see chapter 7). Morgenthaler observes, "More than ever, the church needs to be a refuge for those who have made mistakes and are in pain. And worship needs to be one of the first 'landing places' for these refugees, a place where guilt and hurt can be expressed to God in an atmosphere of loving acceptance."[36]

Interaction is related to the all-important principle of participation in worship. As we saw in chapter 2, there were times in history when participation in worship was strictly relegated to the clergy, with the people largely passive and observing. The Reformation restored participation in worship to the people, but recent history shows that worship is becoming more like a music concert, discarding important elements of congregational participation, such as reciting creeds, celebrating Communion, and saying the Lord's Prayer together.[37] In many churches, even congregational singing is taking a back seat to musical performance in worship. This was an issue as far back as 1995, when Morgenthaler observed, "A renewed commitment to providing interactive worship will be welcomed, not only by regular churchgoers, but by the unchurched—53 percent of whom prefer a worship service that features a lot of participation."[38] In his book, *Worship is a Verb,* Webber urges us to "return worship to the people."[39] Worship should be congregational, involving the entire community, gathered and engaged.

Ultimately, we all need to acknowledge that worship is not just reserved for Sunday morning gatherings. We must cultivate a lifestyle of worship that permeates all areas of our life, inside and outside the church. Risbridger notes: "Throughout Scripture the idea of 'worship' is clearly much broader than singing God's praise; worship is about living the whole of life for the glory of God."[40] The worship of ancient Israel was not strictly confined to the Tabernacle or the Temple. There was no separation of the sacred from the secular. Instead, all of life belonged to God: "The earth is the Lord's, and everything in it" (Ps. 24:1, NIV). The Apostle Paul also understood worship as permeating all of life: "Therefore I urge you, brethren, by the mercies of God, to present your bodies a living and holy sacrifice, acceptable to God, which is your spiritual service of worship" (Rom. 12:1).

This verse comes after Paul's most eloquent explanation of the gospel in the first eleven chapters of Romans. The implication therefore is that living in grateful response to this gospel message involves whole-life worship. Risbridger puts this all in perspective when he mentions a friend who often concludes his services with the song "Come, Now is the Time to Worship,"[41] "because, at the close of the service, the work of worship has only just begun!"[42] Worship that is truly authentic is "whole life" worship. Risbridger mentions this challenge from well-known worship leader, Graham Kendrick, who often poses this question when training other leaders: "What if you were to imagine your role not just as leading this time of worship in your local church, but equipping people to be whole-life worshippers, who can sustain their own spiritual lives the rest of the week?"[43] Both worship leaders and preaching pastors should consider this insightful question when evaluating their overall ministry to the body of Christ.

As worship leaders examine themselves and their commitment to Christ, they would do well to follow the example of the authors of *Doxology and Theology.*[44]

The twelve contributors to this book, all worship leaders from around the United States, unite worship with themes of mission, disciple-making, the Word of God, the Trinity, and family, among other spiritual themes and goals. As the general editor, Matt Boswell, explains, "each of the authors selected for the chapters are faithful men who love the gospel of Christ, and are passionate about serving the local church in worship."[45] They are "thoughtful worship leaders who understand the life-changing marriage between doxology and theology."[46] Boswell speaks for all of the authors when he says, "Since worship leaders are those who lead the people of God in encountering Him in corporate worship, then above all things, we ought to study Him."[47] Thankfully, this shows that there is ample evidence of worship leaders who keep music in right relationship with their commitment to Christ.

In the contemporary Christian music world, it is hard not to find a better example of commitment to Christ above a successful music career than Steven Curtis Chapman. In his memoir, *Between Heaven and the Real World*,[48] Chapman finishes the Prologue with these words:

> While I've woven my life and my story into the songs I've written all these years, my desire has always been to tell the bigger story of God's grace and His faithfulness. With my prayer being, "God, I want to know You and I want to make You known with the gifts You've given me and the life I live," my songs have always come from the places in my journey where I've seen more of who God is and more of my need for Him. I want to tell honest stories and sing songs about how God shows up in our "real world."[49]

Chapman is an excellent example of a highly successful Christian musician who has honored Christ with his music throughout a lifetime of recording and concert ministry, keeping his priorities straight in faithful service to God. There are many other excellent musicians, performing both sacred and secular music, who are equally devoted to Christ and to their music. Their examples inspire us to keep music in proper perspective, not rivaling our devotion to Christ, but enhancing it and giving it a voice.

In conclusion, with these commendable examples in mind, we realize that once all of the tried-and-true personal practices of devotion to God (Bible study, prayer, discipleship, and service) become a regular part of the Christian's lifestyle of worship, music should take its rightful place, subordinate to the Word of God. Music is a good and proper thing, created by God for God's glory, but it should never be an object of worship. Music should point us to the light of Jesus Christ and never to darkness.

The prescription to put music in its proper biblical place is accomplished through coming to terms with our sin and misplaced worship, focusing all our heart's devotion on the one true God. Ultimately, we need to restore the sense of awe to our worship, the same awe that is evidenced by Isaiah's profound encounter with a holy God in Isaiah 6. This worship also must proclaim, sing, and enact the entire story of God's saving acts in history, for the glory of God alone.

As we conclude, I offer these words from Stephen Miller as a suitable benediction: "Christ has appeared to crush our idols under His feet, showing Himself to be the only one worthy of worship. He has put His glory, His mercy, His compassion, and His power on display in bodily form. When we truly see who Christ is and all that He has accomplished for us, how could idols compare? How could we choose to pursue and worship those things?"[50]

NOTES

[1]Con Campbell, *Outreach and the Artist: Sharing the Gospel with the Arts* (Grand Rapids: Zondervan, 2013), 103.

[2]Appreciation to my Cuban friend, Samua Calderon Ramirez, for bringing this passage to my attention for use in this book.

[3]Stephen Miller, *Worship Leaders: We Are Not Rock Stars* (Chicago: Moody Publishers, 2013), 17.

[4]Matt Redman, "The Heart of Worship," © 1997, Thankyou Music.

[5]Jeremy S. Begbie, *Resounding Truth: Christian Wisdom in the World of Music* (Grand Rapids: Baker Academic, 2007), 214.

[6]Ibid.

[7]Ibid., 219.

[8]Campbell, *Outreach and the Artist,* 103-104 (emphasis mine).

[9]John Risbridger, *The Message of Worship: Celebrating the Glory of God in the Whole Life. The Bible Speaks Today,* Derek Tidball, ed. (Downers Grove, IL: InterVarsity Press, 2015), 46.

[10]Timothy Keller, *Counterfeit Gods: The Empty Promises of Money, Sex, and Power, and the Only Hope That Matters* (New York: Penguin Books, 2009), 171.

[11]Harold M. Best, *Music Through the Eyes of Faith* (New York: HarperCollins Publishers, 1993), 50.

[12]D.A. Carson, *Worship by the Book* (Grand Rapids: Zondervan, 2002), 31.

[13]Bruce Ballinger, "We Have Come into His House," © 1976, Universal-MCA Music Publishing, Inc.

[14]Frank S. Page and L. Lavon Gray, *Hungry for Worship: Challenges and Solutions for Today's Church* (Birmingham, AL: New Hope Publishers, 2014), 360.

[15]Ibid.

[16]Marva Dawn, *Reaching Out without Dumbing Down: A Theology of Worship for the Turn-of-the-Century Culture* (Grand Rapids: Eerdmans Publishing Co., 1995), 97.

[17]A.W. Tozer, *Worship: The Reason We Were Created—Collected Insights from A.W. Tozer* (Chicago: Moody Publishers, 2017), 84.

[18]Ibid., 85.

[19]Risbridger, *The Message of Worship,* 129.

[20]Ibid.

[21]Robert E. Webber, *Ancient-Future Worship: Proclaiming and Enacting God's Narrative* (Grand Rapids: Baker Books, 2008).

[22]Ibid., 39-40.

[23]Ibid., 40.

[24]Ibid., 41.

[25]Ibid., 57.

[26]Robert E. Webber, *Worship Old and New* (Grand Rapids: Zondervan, 1994), 149.

[27]Ibid., 150.

[28]Sally Morgenthaler, *Worship Evangelism: Inviting Unbelievers into the Presence of God* (Grand Rapids: Zondervan, 1995).

[29]Ibid., 96-123.

[30]Ibid., 100.

[31]Ibid.

[32]Morgenthaler, *Worship Evangelism,* 101, quoting C.S. Lewis, *Reflections on the Psalms* (New York: Harcourt, Brace, Jovanovich, 1958), 93.

[33]Ibid, 102.

[34]Ibid.

[35]Ibid., 110.

[36]Ibid., 112.

[37]Ibid., 117.

[38]Ibid., 118.

[39]Robert E. Webber, *Worship is a Verb: Eight Principles for Transforming Worship* (Peabody, MA: Hendrickson Publishers, Inc., 1992), 152.

[40]Risbridger, *The Message of Worship,* 87.

[41]Brian Doerksen, "Come, Now is the Time to Worship," © 1998, Vineyard Songs.

[42]Risbridger, *The Message of Worship,* 162.

[43]Ibid., 163.

[44]Matt Boswell, ed., *Doxology and Theology: How the Gospel Forms the Worship Leader* (Nashville: B&H Publishing Group, 2013).

[45]Ibid., 3.

[46]Ibid., 1.

[47]Ibid., 2.

[48]Steven Curtis Chapman with Ken Abraham, *Between Heaven and the Real World: My Story* (Grand Rapids: Revell, 2017).

[49]Ibid., 17.

[50]Miller, *Worship Leaders,* 34.

Appendix 1

Selected Scriptures on Idolatry[1]

Denunciations Against Idolatry

Genesis 35:2
So Jacob said to his household and to all who were with him, "Put away the foreign gods which are among you, and purify yourselves and change your garments;"

Exodus 20:3
You shall have no other gods before Me.

Exodus 20:4-6
You shall not make for yourself an idol, or any likeness of what is in heaven above or on the earth beneath or in the water under the earth. You shall not worship them or serve them; for I, the LORD your God, am a jealous God, visiting the iniquity of the fathers on the children, on the third and the fourth generations of those who hate Me, but showing lovingkindness to thousands, to those who love Me and keep My commandments.

Exodus 20:23
You shall not make *other gods* besides Me; gods of silver or gods of gold, you shall not make for yourselves.

Exodus 23:13
Now concerning everything which I have said to you, be on your guard; and do not mention the name of other gods, nor let *them* be heard from your mouth.

Exodus 34:17
You shall make for yourself no molten gods.

Leviticus 19:4
Do not turn to idols or make for yourselves molten gods; I am the LORD your God.

Leviticus 26:1
You shall not make for yourselves idols, nor shall you set up for yourselves an image or a *sacred* pillar, nor shall you place a figured stone in your land to bow down to it; for I am the LORD your God.

Leviticus 26:30
I then will destroy your high places, and cut down your incense altars, and heap your remains on the remains of your idols, for My soul shall abhor you.

Deuteronomy 4:15-19
So watch yourselves carefully, since you did not see any form on the day the LORD spoke to you at Horeb from the midst of the fire, so that you do not act corruptly and make a graven image for yourselves in the form of any figure, the likeness of male or female, the likeness of any animal that is on the earth, the likeness of any winged bird that flies in the sky, the likeness of anything that creeps on the ground, the likeness of any fish that is in the water below the earth. And *beware* not to lift up your eyes to heaven and see the sun and the moon and the stars, all the host of heaven, and be drawn away and worship them and serve them, those which the LORD your God has allotted to all the peoples under the whole heaven.

Deuteronomy 4:23
So watch yourselves, that you do not forget the covenant of the LORD your God which He made with you, and make for yourselves a graven image in the form of anything *against* which the LORD your God has commanded you.

Deuteronomy 4:25-28
When you become the father of children and children's children and have remained long in the land, and act corruptly, and make an idol in the form of anything, and do that which is evil in the sight of the LORD your God *so as* to provoke Him to anger, I call heaven and earth to witness against you today, that you will surely perish quickly from the land where you are going over the Jordan to possess it. You shall not live long on it, but will be utterly destroyed. The LORD will scatter you among the peoples, and you will be left few in number among the nations where the LORD drives you. There you will serve gods, the work of man's hands, wood and stone, which neither see nor hear nor eat nor smell.

Deuteronomy 5:7
You shall have no other gods before Me.

Deuteronomy 5:8-9
You shall not make for yourself an idol, *or* any likeness *of* what is in heaven above or on the earth beneath or in the water under the earth. You shall not worship them or serve them; for I, the LORD your God, am a jealous God, visiting the iniquity of the fathers on the children, and on the third and the fourth *generations* of those who hate Me,

Deuteronomy 11:16-17
Beware that your hearts are not deceived, and that you do not turn away and serve other gods and worship them. Or the anger of the LORD will be kindled against you, and He will shut up the heavens so that there will be no rain and the ground will not yield its fruit; and you will perish quickly from the good land which the LORD is giving you.

Deuteronomy 11:28
and the curse, if you do not listen to the commandments of the LORD your God, but turn aside from the way which I am commanding you today, by following other gods which you have not known.

Deuteronomy 12:31
You shall not behave thus toward the LORD your God, for every abominable act which the LORD hates they have done for their gods; for they even burn their sons and daughters in the fire to their gods.

Deuteronomy 16:21-22
You shall not plant for yourself an Asherah of any kind of tree beside the altar of the LORD your God, which you shall make for yourself. You shall not set up for yourself a *sacred* pillar which the LORD your God hates.

Deuteronomy 27:15
Cursed is the man who makes an idol or a molten image, an abomination to the LORD, the work of the hands of the craftsman, and sets *it* up in secret. And all the people shall answer and say, "Amen."

Deuteronomy 30:17-18
But if your heart turns away and you will not obey, but are drawn away and worship other gods and serve them, I declare to you today that you shall surely perish. You will not prolong *your* days in the land where you are crossing the Jordan to enter and possess it.

Deuteronomy 31:16-18
The LORD said to Moses, "Behold, you are about to lie down with your fathers; and this people will arise and play the harlot with the strange gods of the land, into the midst of which they are going, and will forsake Me and break My covenant which I have made with them. Then My anger will be kindled against them in that day, and I will forsake them and hide My face from them, and they will be consumed, and

many evils and troubles will come upon them; so that they will say in that day, 'Is it not because our God is not among us that these evils have come upon us?' But I will surely hide My face in that day because of all the evil which they will do, for they will turn to other gods.'"

Deuteronomy 31:19-21
Now therefore, write this song for yourselves, and teach it to the sons of Israel; put it on their lips, so that this song may be a witness for Me against the sons of Israel. For when I bring them into the land flowing with milk and honey, which I swore to their fathers, and they have eaten and are satisfied and become prosperous, then they will turn to other gods and serve them, and spurn Me and break My covenant. Then it shall come about, when many evils and troubles have come upon them, that this song will testify before them as a witness (for it shall not be forgotten from the lips of their descendants); for I know their intent which they are developing today, before I have brought them into the land which I swore.

Deuteronomy 32:15-18
But Jeshurun grew fat and kicked—
You are grown fat, thick, and sleek—
Then he forsook God who made him,
And scorned the Rock of his salvation.
They made Him jealous with strange *gods;*
With abominations they provoked Him to anger.
They sacrificed to demons who were not God,
To gods whom they have not known,
New *gods* who came lately,
Whom your fathers did not dread.
You neglected the Rock who begot you,
And forgot the God who gave you birth.

Deuteronomy 32:19-22
The LORD saw *this,* and spurned *them*
Because of the provocation of His sons and daughters.
Then He said, "I will hide My face from them,
I will see what their end *shall be;*
For they are a perverse generation,
Sons in whom is no faithfulness.
They have made Me jealous with *what* is not God;
They have provoked Me to anger with their idols.

So I will make them jealous with *those who* are not a people;
I will provoke them to anger with a foolish nation,
For a fire is kindled in My anger,
And burns to the lowest part of Sheol,
And consumes the earth with its yield,
And sets on fire the foundations of the mountains."

Deuteronomy 32:23-26
I will heap misfortunes on them;
I will use My arrows on them.
They will be wasted by famine, and consumed by plague
And bitter destruction;
And the teeth of beasts I will send upon them,
With the venom of crawling things of the dust.
Outside the sword will bereave,
And inside terror—
Both young man and virgin,
The nursling with the man of gray hair.
I would have said, "I will cut them to pieces,
I will remove the memory of them from men,"

1 Samuel 15:23
For rebellion is as the sin of divination,
And insubordination is as iniquity and idolatry.
Because you have rejected the word of the LORD,
He has also rejected you from *being* king.

1 Kings 9:6-9
But if you or your sons indeed turn away from following Me, and do not keep My commandments and My statutes which I have set before you, and go and serve other gods and worship them, then I will cut off Israel from the land which I have given them, and the house which I have consecrated for My name, I will cast out of My sight. So Israel will become a proverb and a byword among all peoples. And this house will become a heap of ruins; everyone who passes by will be astonished and hiss and say, "Why has the LORD done thus to this land and to this house?" And they will say, "Because they forsook the LORD their God, who brought their fathers out of the land of Egypt, and adopted other gods and worshiped them and served them, therefore the LORD has brought all this adversity on them."

Job 31:26-28
If I have looked at the sun when it shone
Or the moon going in splendor,
And my heart became secretly enticed,
And my hand threw a kiss from my mouth,
That too would have been an iniquity *calling for* judgment,
For I would have denied God above.

Psalm 16:4
The sorrows of those who have bartered for another *god* will be multiplied;
I shall not pour out their drink offerings of blood,
Nor will I take their names upon my lips.

Psalm 44:20-21
If we had forgotten the name of our God
Or extended our hands to a strange god,
Would not God find this out?
For He knows the secrets of the heart.

Psalm 81:9
Let there be no strange god among you;
Nor shall you worship any foreign god.

Psalm 97:7
Let all those be ashamed who serve graven images,
Who boast themselves of idols;
Worship Him, all you gods.

Isaiah 42:17
They will be turned back *and* be utterly put to shame,
Who trust in idols,
Who say to molten images,
"You are our gods."

Isaiah 45:16
They will be put to shame and even humiliated, all of them;
The manufacturers of idols will go away together in humiliation.

Jonah 2:8
Those who regard vain idols
Forsake their faithfulness,

Habakkuk 1:16
Therefore they offer a sacrifice to their net
And burn incense to their fishing net;
Because through these things their catch is large,
And their food is plentiful.

Acts 17:16
Now while Paul was waiting for them at Athens, his spirit was being provoked within him as he was observing the city full of idols.

Romans 1:25
For they exchanged the truth of God for a lie, and worshiped and served the creature rather than the Creator, who is blessed forever. Amen.

1 Corinthians 6:9-10
Or do you not know that the unrighteous will not inherit the kingdom of God? Do not be deceived; neither fornicators, nor idolaters, nor adulterers, nor effeminate, nor homosexuals, nor thieves, nor *the* covetous, nor drunkards, nor revilers, nor swindlers, will inherit the kingdom of God.

1 Corinthians 10:7
Do not be idolaters, as some of them were; as it is written, "THE PEOPLE SAT DOWN TO EAT AND DRINK, AND STOOD UP TO PLAY."

1 Corinthians 10:14
Therefore, my beloved, flee from idolatry.

1 John 5:21
Little children, guard yourselves from idols.

Revelation 21:8
But for the cowardly and unbelieving and abominable and murderers and immoral persons and sorcerers and idolaters and all liars, their part *will be* in the lake that burns with fire and brimstone, which is the second death.

Revelation 22:15
Outside are the dogs and the sorcerers and the immoral persons and the murderers and the idolaters, and everyone who loves and practices lying.

Folly of Idolatry

Exodus 32:20
He took the calf which they had made and burned *it* with fire, and ground it to powder, and scattered it over the surface of the water and made the sons of Israel drink *it.*

Deuteronomy 4:28
There you will serve gods, the work of man's hands, wood and stone, which neither see nor hear nor eat nor smell.

Deuteronomy 32:37-38
And He will say, "Where are their gods,
The rock in which they sought refuge?
Who ate the fat of their sacrifices,
And drank the wine of their drink offering?
Let them rise up and help you,
Let them be your hiding place!"

Judges 6:31
But Joash said to all who stood against him, "Will you contend for Baal, or will you deliver him? Whoever will plead for him shall be put to death by morning. If he is a god, let him contend for himself, because someone has torn down his altar."

Judges 10:14
Go and cry out to the gods which you have chosen; let them deliver you in the time of your distress.

1 Samuel 5:3-4
When the Ashdodites arose early the next morning, behold, Dagon had fallen on his face to the ground before the ark of the LORD. So they took Dagon and set him in his place again. But when they arose early the next morning, behold, Dagon had fallen on his face to the ground before the ark of the LORD. And the head of Dagon and both the palms of his hands *were* cut off on the threshold; only the trunk of Dagon was left to him.

1 Kings 18:27
It came about at noon, that Elijah mocked them and said, "Call out with a loud voice, for he is a god; either he is occupied or gone aside, or is on a journey, or perhaps he is asleep and needs to be awakened."

2 Kings 19:18
and have cast their gods into the fire, for they were not gods but the work of men's hands, wood and stone. So they have destroyed them.

2 Chronicles 25:15
Then the anger of the LORD burned against Amaziah, and He sent him a prophet who said to him, "Why have you sought the gods of the people who have not delivered their own people from your hand?"

2 Chronicles 28:22-23
Now in the time of his distress this same King Ahaz became yet more unfaithful to the LORD. For he sacrificed to the gods of Damascus which had defeated him, and said, "Because the gods of the kings of Aram helped them, I will sacrifice to them that they may help me." But they became the downfall of him and all Israel.

Psalm 96:5
For all the gods of the peoples are idols,
But the LORD made the heavens.

Psalm 106:20
Thus they exchanged their glory
For the image of an ox that eats grass.

Psalm 115:4-5
Their idols are silver and gold,
The work of man's hands.
They have mouths, but they cannot speak;
They have eyes, but they cannot see;

Psalm 115:8
Those who make them will become like them,
Everyone who trusts in them.

Psalm 135:15-18
The idols of the nations are *but* silver and gold,
The work of man's hands.
They have mouths, but they do not speak;
They have eyes, but they do not see;
They have ears, but they do not hear,
Nor is there any breath at all in their mouths.

Those who make them will be like them,
Yes, everyone who trusts in them.

Isaiah 2:8
Their land has also been filled with idols;
They worship the work of their hands,
That which their fingers have made.

Isaiah 16:12
So it will come about when Moab presents himself,
When he wearies himself upon *his* high place
And comes to his sanctuary to pray,
That he will not prevail.

Isaiah 36:18
Beware that Hezekiah does not mislead you, saying, "The LORD will deliver us." Has any one of the gods of the nations delivered his land from the hand of the king of Assyria?

Isaiah 37:19
and have cast their gods into the fire, for they were not gods but the work of men's hands, wood and stone. So they have destroyed them.

Isaiah 40:19-20
As for the idol, a craftsman casts it,
A goldsmith plates it with gold,
And a silversmith *fashions* chains of silver.
He who is too impoverished for *such* an offering
Selects a tree that does not rot;
He seeks out for himself a skillful craftsman
To prepare an idol that will not totter.

Isaiah 41:23-24
Declare the things that are going to come afterward,
That we may know that you are gods;
Indeed, do good or evil, that we may anxiously look about us and fear together.
Behold, you are of no account,
And your work amounts to nothing;
He who chooses you is an abomination.

Isaiah 41:26-29
Who has declared *this* from the beginning, that we might know?
Or from former times, that we may say, "*He is* right!"?
Surely there was no one who declared,
Surely there was no one who proclaimed,
Surely there was no one who heard your words.
Formerly *I said* to Zion, Behold, here they are."
And to Jerusalem, "I will give a messenger of good news."
But when I look, there is no one,
And there is no counselor among them
Who, if I ask, can give an answer.
Behold, all of them are false;
Their works are worthless,
Their molten images are wind and emptiness.

Isaiah 44:9-20
Those who fashion a graven image are all of them futile, and their precious things are of no profit; even their own witnesses fail to see or know, so that they will be put to shame. Who has fashioned a god or cast an idol to no profit? Behold, all his companions will be put to shame, for the craftsmen themselves are mere men. Let them all assemble themselves, let them stand up, let them tremble, let them together be put to shame.

The man shapes iron into a cutting tool and does his work over the coals, fashioning it with hammers and working it with his strong arm. He also gets hungry and his strength fails; he drinks no water and becomes weary. *Another* shapes wood, he extends a measuring line; he outlines it with red chalk. He works it with planes and outlines it with a compass, and makes it like the form of a man, like the beauty of man, so that it may sit in a house. Surely he cuts cedars for himself, and takes a cypress or an oak and raises *it* for himself among the trees of the forest. He plants a fir, and the rain makes it grow. Then it becomes *something* for a man to burn, so he takes one of them and warms himself; he also makes a fire to bake bread. He also makes a god and worships it; he makes it a graven image and falls down before it. Half of it he burns in the fire; over *this* half he eats meat as he roasts a roast and is satisfied. He also warms himself and says, "Aha! I am warm, I have seen the fire." But the rest of it he makes into a god, his graven image. He falls down before it and worships; he also prays to it and says, "Deliver me, for you are my god."

They do not know, nor do they understand, for He has smeared over their eyes so that they cannot see and their hearts so that they cannot comprehend. No one recalls, nor is there knowledge or understanding to say, "I have burned half of it in the fire and also have baked bread over its coals. I roast meat and eat *it.* Then I make the rest of it into an abomination, I fall down before a block of wood!" He feeds on ashes; a deceived heart has turned him aside. And he cannot deliver himself, nor say, "Is there not a lie in my right hand?"

Isaiah 45:20
Gather yourselves and come;
Draw near together, you fugitives of the nations;
They have no knowledge,
Who carry about their wooden idol
And pray to a god who cannot save.

Isaiah 46:1-2
Bel has bowed down, Nebo stoops over;
Their images are *consigned* to the beasts and the cattle.
The things that you carry are burdensome,
A load for the weary *beast.*
They stooped over, they have bowed down together;
They could not rescue the burden,
But have themselves gone into captivity.

Isaiah 46:7
They lift it upon the shoulder *and* carry it;
They set it in its place and it stands *there.*
It does not move from its place.
Though one may cry to it, it cannot answer;
It cannot deliver him from his distress.

Isaiah 47:12-15
Stand *fast* now in your spells
And in your many sorceries
With which you have labored from your youth;
Perhaps you will be able to profit,
Perhaps you may cause trembling.
You are wearied with your many counsels;
Let now the astrologers,
Those who prophesy by the stars,
Those who predict by the new moons,
Stand up and save you from what will come upon you.

Behold, they have become like stubble,
Fire burns them;
They cannot deliver themselves from the power of the flame;
There will be no coal to warm by
Nor a fire to sit before!
So have those become to you with whom you have labored,
Who have trafficked with you from your youth;
Each has wandered in his own way;
There is none to save you.

Isaiah 57:13
When you cry out, let your collection *of idols* deliver you.
But the wind will carry all of them up,
And a breath will take *them away.*
But he who takes refuge in Me will inherit the land
And will possess My holy mountain."

Jeremiah 2:28
But where are your gods
Which you made for yourself?
Let them arise, if they can save you
In the time of your trouble;
For *according to* the number of your cities
Are your gods, O Judah.

Jeremiah 10:3-16
For the customs of the peoples are delusion;
Because it is wood cut from the forest,
The work of the hands of a craftsman with a cutting tool.
They decorate *it* with silver and with gold;
They fasten it with nails and with hammers
So that it will not totter.
Like a scarecrow in a cucumber field are they,
And they cannot speak;
They must be carried,
Because they cannot walk!
Do not fear them,
For they can do no harm,
Nor can they do any good."

There is none like You, O LORD;
You are great, and great is Your name in might.
Who would not fear You, O King of the nations?
Indeed it is Your due!
For among all the wise men of the nations
And in all their kingdoms,
There is none like You.
But they are altogether stupid and foolish
In their discipline of delusion — their idol is wood!
Beaten silver is brought from Tarshish,
And gold from Uphaz,
The work of a craftsman and of the hands of a goldsmith;
Violet and purple are their clothing;
They are all the work of skilled men.
But the LORD is the true God;
He is the living God and the everlasting King.
At His wrath the earth quakes,
And the nations cannot endure His indignation.

Thus you shall say to them, "The gods that did not make the heavens and the earth will perish from the earth and from under the heavens."

It is He who made the earth by His power,
Who established the world by His wisdom;
And by His understanding He has stretched out the heavens.
When He utters His voice, *there is* a tumult of waters in the heavens,
And He causes the clouds to ascend from the end of the earth;
He makes lightning for the rain,
And brings out the wind from His storehouses.
Every man is stupid, devoid of knowledge;
Every goldsmith is put to shame by his idols;
For his molten images are deceitful,
And there is no breath in them.
They are worthless, a work of mockery;
In the time of their punishment they will perish.
The portion of Jacob is not like these;
For the Maker of all is He,
And Israel is the tribe of His inheritance;
The LORD of hosts is His name.

Jeremiah 11:12
Then the cities of Judah and the inhabitants of Jerusalem will go and cry to the gods to whom they burn incense, but they surely will not save them in the time of their disaster.

Jeremiah 14:22
Are there any among the idols of the nations who give rain?
Or can the heavens grant showers?
Is it not You, O LORD our God?
Therefore we hope in You,
For You are the one who has done all these things.

Jeremiah 16:19-20
O LORD, my strength and my stronghold,
And my refuge in the day of distress,
To You the nations will come
From the ends of the earth and say,
Our fathers have inherited nothing but falsehood,
Futility and things of no profit."
Can man make gods for himself?
Yet they are not gods!

Jeremiah 48:13
And Moab will be ashamed of Chemosh, as the house of Israel was ashamed of Bethel, their confidence.

Jeremiah 51:17
All mankind is stupid, devoid of knowledge;
Every goldsmith is put to shame by his idols,
For his molten images are deceitful,
And there is no breath in them.

Daniel 5:23
but you have exalted yourself against the Lord of heaven; and they have brought the vessels of His house before you, and you and your nobles, your wives and your concubines have been drinking wine from them; and you have praised the gods of silver and gold, of bronze, iron, wood and stone, which do not see, hear or understand. But the God in whose hand are your life-breath and all your ways, you have not glorified.

Hosea 8:5-6
He has rejected your calf, O Samaria, *saying,*
"My anger burns against them!"
How long will they be incapable of innocence?
For from Israel is even this!
A craftsman made it, so it is not God;
Surely the calf of Samaria will be broken to pieces.

Habakkuk 2:18-19
What profit is the idol when its maker has carved it,
Or an image, a teacher of falsehood?
For *its* maker trusts in his *own* handiwork
When he fashions speechless idols.
Woe to him who says to a *piece of* wood, "Awake!"
To a mute stone, "Arise!"
And that is *your* teacher?
Behold, it is overlaid with gold and silver,
And there is no breath at all inside it.

Zechariah 10:2
For the teraphim speak iniquity,
And the diviners see lying visions
And tell false dreams;
They comfort in vain.
Therefore *the people* wander like sheep,
They are afflicted, because there is no shepherd.

Acts 14:15
Men, why are you doing these things? We are also men of the same nature as you, and preach the gospel to you that you should turn from these vain things to a living God, who made the heaven and the earth and the sea and all that is in them.

Acts 17:22-23
So Paul stood in the midst of the Areopagus and said, "Men of Athens, I observe that you are very religious in all respects. For while I was passing through and examining the objects of your worship, I also found an altar with this inscription, 'TO AN UNKNOWN GOD.' Therefore what you worship in ignorance, this I proclaim to you."

Acts 17:29
Being then the children of God, we ought not to think that the Divine Nature is like gold or silver or stone, an image formed by the art and thought of man.

Romans 1:22-23
Professing to be wise, they became fools, and exchanged the glory of the incorruptible God for an image in the form of corruptible man and of birds and four-footed animals and crawling creatures.

1 Corinthians 8:4-5
Therefore concerning the eating of things sacrificed to idols, we know that there is no such thing as an idol in the world, and that there is no God but one. For even if there are so-called gods whether in heaven or on earth, as indeed there are many gods and many lords,

1 Corinthians 10:19
What do I mean then? That a thing sacrificed to idols is anything, or that an idol is anything?

1 Corinthians 12:2
You know that when you were pagans, *you were* led astray to the mute idols, however you were led.

Galatians 4:8
However at that time, when you did not know God, you were slaves to those which by nature are no gods.

Revelation 9:20
The rest of mankind, who were not killed by these plagues, did not repent of the works of their hands, so as not to worship demons, and the idols of gold and of silver and of brass and of stone and of wood, which can neither see nor hear nor walk;

NOTE

[1]Scripture references identified in Orville J. Nave, *Nave's Topical Bible: A Digest of the Holy Scriptures* (McLean, VA: MacDonald Publishing Co., 2002).

Appendix 2

Directory of Psalm Literary Types[1]

Hymn: 8, 19, 29, 33, 36, 46–48, 66, 76, 84, 87, 89, 93, 95–100, 103–104, 111, 113–114, 117, 122, 145–150
Community Lament: 12, 44, 58, 60, 74, 79–80, 83, 85, 90, 94, 123, 126, 129, 137
Individual Lament: 3–7, 9–10, 13, 14, 17, 22, 25–28, 31, 35, 38–43, 51–52, 53, 54–57, 59, 61, 64, 69–71, 77, 86, 88–89, 102, 108–109, 120, 130, 139–143
Community Song of Thanksgiving: 65, 67, 75, 107–108, 124
Individual Song of Thanksgiving: 18, 30, 32, 34, 40, 66, 92, 116, 118, 138
Wisdom/Torah: 1, 19, 36–37, 49, 73, 112, 119, 127–128, 133
Songs of Trust: 11, 16, 23, 27, 62–63, 91, 121, 125, 131
Royal: 2, 20–21, 45, 72, 89, 101, 110, 132, 144
Liturgy: 15, 24, 50, 68, 81–82, 115, 132, 134
Remembrance or Storytelling: 78, 105–106, 135–136

NOTE

[1]Type listings identified in Andrew E. Hill, "Catalog of Psalmic Types," *Enter His Courts with Praise! Old Testament Worship for the New Testament Church* (Ada, MI: Baker Books, 1997), 199-200.

Bibliography

Beale, G.K. *We Become What We Worship: A Biblical Theology of Idolatry.* Downers Grove, IL: IVP Academic, 2008.

Begbie, Jeremy S. *Resounding Truth: Christian Wisdom in the World of Music.* Grand Rapids: Baker Academic, 2007.

Best, Harold M. *Music Through the Eyes of Faith.* New York: HarperCollins Publishers, 1993.

________. *Unceasing Worship: Biblical Perspectives on Worship and the Arts.* Downers Grove, IL: InterVarsity Press, 2003.

Block, Daniel I. *For the Glory of God: Recovering a Biblical Theology of Worship.* Grand Rapids: Baker Academic, 2014.

Boswell, Matt, ed. *Doxology and Theology: How the Gospel Forms the Worship Leader.* Nashville: B&H Publishing Group, 2013.

Braun, Joachim. *Music in Ancient Israel/Palestine: Archaeological, Written, and Comparative Sources.* Grand Rapids: Eerdmans Publishing Co., 2002.

Bruce, F.F. *1 and 2 Thessalonians.* Vol. 45, *Word Biblical Commentary.* Nashville: Thomas Nelson, 1982.

Campbell, Con. *Outreach and the Artist: Sharing the Gospel with the Arts.* Grand Rapids: Zondervan, 2013.

Caram, Daniel G. *Tabernacle of David.* Longwood, FL: Xulon Press, 2003.

Carson D.A. *Worship by the Book.* Grand Rapids: Zondervan, 2002.

Chapman, Steven Curtis with Ken Abraham. *Between Heaven and the Real World: My Story.* Grand Rapids: Revell, 2017.

Conner, Kevin J. *The Tabernacle of David.* Portland, OR: City Bible Publishing, 1989.

Copan, Paul and William Lane Craig. *Creation Out of Nothing: A Biblical, Philosophical, and Scientific Exploration.* Grand Rapids: Baker Academic, 2004.

Dawn, Marva. *Reaching Out without Dumbing Down: A Theology of Worship for the Turn-of-the-Century Culture.* Grand Rapids: Eerdmans Publishing Co., 1995.

Ellis, Larry. *Radical Worship: What Sunday Morning Can Never Give You.* Denver, CO: Adoration Publishing Co., 2014.

Foley, Edward. *Foundations of Christian Music: The Music of Pre-Constantinian Christianity.* Collegeville, MN: Liturgical Press, 1996.

Grout, Donald Jay. *A History of Western Music.* Revised Edition. New York: W.W. Norton and Co., Inc., 1960.

Hedrick, Brian L. *The Biblical Foundations of Instrumental Music in Worship: Four Pillars.* Denver, CO: Outskirts Press, 2009.

Hill, Andrew E. *Baker's Handbook of Bible Lists.* Grand Rapids: Baker Books, 1981.

________. *Enter His Courts with Praise! Old Testament Worship for the New Testament Church.* Grand Rapids: Baker Books, 1996.

Hurtado, Larry W. *At the Origins of Christian Worship.* Grand Rapids: Eerdmans Publishing Co., 1999.

Hustad, Donald P. "Music in the Worship of the New Testament." In *Music and the Arts in Christian Worship,* ed. Robert E. Webber, 192-195. Vol. 4, Book 1, *The Complete Library of Christian Worship.* Nashville: Star Song, 1994.

________. "Music in the Worship of the Old Testament." In *Music and the Arts in Christian Worship,* ed. Robert E. Webber, 188-192. Vol. 4, Book 1, *The Complete Library of Christian Worship.* Nashville: Star Song, 1994.

Jones, Paul S. *Singing and Making Music: Issues in Church Music Today.* Phillipsburg, NJ: P&R Publishing, 2006.

Jordan, James. *The Musician's Soul.* Chicago: GIA Publications, Inc., 1999.

Kavanaugh, Patrick. *Spiritual Lives of the Great Composers.* Revised and Expanded. Grand Rapids: Zondervan, 1996.

Keller, Timothy. *Counterfeit Gods: The Empty Promises of Money, Sex, and Power, and the Only Hope That Matters.* New York: Penguin Books, 2009.

Kidd, Reggie M. *With One Voice: Discovering Christ's Song in Our Worship.* Grand Rapids: Baker Books, 2005.

Leithart, Peter J. *From Silence to Song: The Davidic Liturgical Revolution.* Moscow, ID: Canon Press, 2003.

Lints, Richard. *Identity and Idolatry: The Image of God and Its Inversion.* Downers Grove, IL: InterVarsity Press, 2015.

McPherson, Brennan S. *Flood: The Story of Noah and the Family Who Raised Him.* Sparta, WI: McPherson Publishing, 2017.

Mendl, R.W.S. *The Divine Quest in Music.* London: Rockliff Publishing, 1957.

Miller, Stephen. *Worship Leaders: We Are Not Rock Stars.* Chicago: Moody Publishers, 2013.

Montagu, Jeremy. "*How Music and Instruments Began: A Brief Overview of the Origin and Entire Development of Music, from Its Earliest Stages.*" *Frontiers in Sociology* 2:8. doi: 103389/fsoc.2017.00008, 2017.

Morgenthaler, Sally. *Worship Evangelism: Inviting Unbelievers into the Presence of God.* Grand Rapids: Zondervan, 1995.

Morley, Iain. *The Prehistory of Music: Human Evolution, Archaeology, and the Origins of Musicality.* Oxford: Oxford University Press, 2013.

Mowinckel, Sigmund. *The Psalms in Israel's Worship.* Grand Rapids: Eerdmans Publishing Co., 2004.

Myers, Robert A. *Strategic Portraits: People and Movements That Shaped Evangelical Worship.* Jacksonville, FL: Webber Institute Books, 2019.

Myers, Robert Manson. *Handel's Messiah: A Touchstone of Taste.* New York: Octagon Books, 1971.

Nave, Orville J. *Nave's Topical Bible: A Digest of the Holy Scriptures.* McLean, VA: MacDonald Publishing, 2002.

Noland, Rory. *The Heart of the Artist: A Character-Building Guide for You and Your Ministry Team.* Zondervan, 1999.

Page, Frank S. and L. Lavon Gray. *Hungry for Worship: Challenges and Solutions for Today's Church.* Birmingham, AL: New Hope Publishers, 2014.

Redlick, Hans Ferdinand. *Bruckner and Mahler.* London: J.M. Dent Ltd., 1955.

Risbridger, John. *The Message of Worship: Celebrating the Glory of God in the Whole Life. The Bible Speaks Today,* Derek Tidball, ed. Downers Grove, IL: InterVarsity Press, 2015.

Ross, Allen P. *A Commentary on the Psalms,* 3 vols. Grand Rapids: Kregal Academic, 2016.

________. *Recalling the Hope of Glory: Biblical Worship from the Garden to the New Creation.* Grand Rapids: Kregel Publications, 2006.

Seel, Thomas Allen. *A Theology of Music for Worship Derived from the Book of Revelation.* Metuchen, NJ: Scarecrow Press, Inc., 1995.

Speed, A.C. "Jared Leto has started a CULT on an island and his followers call him 'Prophet.'" Raw Music TV: Music, News, Gaming and Culture, Sept. 18, 2019. Accessed Sept. 23, 2019. https://www.rawmusictv.com/article/amp/2019/Jared-Leto-has-started-a-CULT-on-an-island-and-his-followers-call-him-Prophet.

Spurgeon, Charles H. *The Treasury of David.* Peabody, MA: Hendrickson Publishers, 1988.

Stapert, Calvin R. *A New Song for an Old World: Musical Thought in the Early Church.* Grand Rapids: Eerdmans Publishing Co., 2007.

Taylor, W. David O. *Glimpses of the New Creation: Worship and the Formative Power of the Arts.* Grand Rapids: Eerdmans Publishing Co., 2019.

Terry, Thomas J. and J. Ryan Lister, *Images and Idols: Creativity for the Christian Life.* Chicago: Moody Publishers, 2018.

Tomlinson, Gary. *A Million Years of Music: The Emergence of Human Modernity.* Brooklyn, NY: Zone Books, 2015.

Tozer, A.W. *Worship: The Reason We Were Created—Collected Insights from A.W. Tozer.* Chicago: Moody Publishers, 2017.

Vasicek, Ed. "Do you think music has become an idol in our churches?" Sharper Iron, March 26, 2014. Accessed Nov. 1, 2019. https://sharperiron.org/forum/poll-do-you-think-music-has-become-idol-our-churches.

Wainwright, Geoffrey and Karen B. Westerfield Tucker. *The Oxford History of Christian Worship.* New York: Oxford University Press, 2006.

Warren, Rick. *The Purpose Driven Life: What on Earth Am I Here For?* Grand Rapids: Zondervan, 2012.

Webber, Robert E. *Ancient-Future Worship: Proclaiming and Enacting God's Narrative.* Grand Rapids: Baker Books, 2008.

________. *The Divine Embrace: Recovering the Passionate Spiritual Life.* Grand Rapids: Baker Books, 2006.

________. *Worship Is a Verb: Eight Principles for Transforming Worship.* Peabody, MA: Hendrickson Publishers, Inc., 1992.

________. *Worship Old and New.* Grand Rapids: Zondervan, 1994.

Webber, Robert E., ed. *Music and the Arts in Christian Worship,* Vol. 4, Book 1, *The Complete Library of Christian Worship.* Nashville: Star Song, 1994.

________. *The Biblical Foundations of Christian Worship,* Vol. 1, *The Complete Library of Christian Worship.* Nashville: Star Song, 1994.

White, James F. *A Brief History of Christian Worship.* Nashville: Abingdon Press, 1993.

White, Susan J. *Foundations of Christian Worship.* Louisville, KY: Westminster John Knox Press, 2006.

Witvliet, John D. *The Biblical Psalms in Christian Worship: A Brief Introduction and Guide to Resources.* Grand Rapids: Eerdmans Publishing Co., 2007.

Wooten, Victor L. *The Music Lesson: A Spiritual Search for Growth Through Music.* New York: Berkley Books, 2006.

Wright, C.J.H. *The Mission of God.* Downers Grove, IL: InterVarsity Press, 2006.

Wright, N.T. *Simply Christian: Why Christianity Makes Sense.* New York: Harper One, 2006.

About the Author

Brian Hedrick was exposed to music at a fairly early age, patiently enduring piano lessons in elementary school, taking advantage of an elementary school band program, and learning to play the trumpet. Upon entering junior high, he was given the option either to be one of several French horn players or one of many trumpet players; he made a choice that would impact the rest of his life.

Playing the French horn through junior high, high school, and college—and even meeting his wife in the French horn section in the college marching band—he had every reason to have an elevated view of music. But as he approached college graduation, through the influence of the home church of his wife-to-be, he made the decision to surrender his life to Christ, and was eventually called into full-time music ministry.

Brian Hedrick is a graduate of Florida State University (BME, 1981), Southwestern Baptist Theological Seminary (MM, 1985), and the Robert E. Webber Institute for Worship Studies (DWS, 2008). He has served churches in Texas, Arizona, and Georgia, and has been the assistant pastor for instrumental music at Johnson Ferry Baptist Church in Marietta, Georgia, since 1994, where he is also director of the Johnson Ferry Conservatory for the Arts.

Johnson Ferry Baptist Church averages about 4,000 worshipers between its five Sunday services. Brian directs four groups that participate regularly in worship: the 50-plus-member Johnson Ferry Orchestra, the 20-piece Gospel Jazz Band, the 5-octave Bells of Johnson Ferry, and the 40-piece Youth Orchestra.

The Johnson Ferry Conservatory for the Arts offers private music lessons and art classes to the community in a Christian environment. More than 150 students are enrolled, studying music and art under the leadership of more than a dozen teachers.

Brian has published three arrangements for church orchestra and one book, *The Biblical Foundations of Instrumental Music in Worship: Four Pillars* (Outskirts Press, 2009). He is a member of the Metro Instrumental Directors Conference, and hosted the annual meeting of church instrumental directors from around the country in 2018. Brian and his wife Mellonee have four children and five grandchildren.

CPSIA information can be obtained
at www.ICGtesting.com
Printed in the USA
JSHW020139221220
10402JS00003B/16